bake it better

70 Show-Stopping Recipes to Level Up Your Baking Skills

PHOTOGRAPHY BY SAM A. HARRIS

matt adlard

bake it better

70 Show-Stopping Recipes to Level Up Your Baking Skills

DK | Penguin Random House

Publisher Mike Sanders
Senior Editor Molly Ahuja
Art Director William Thomas
Senior Designer Jessica Lee
Photographer Sam A. Harris
Food Stylists Holly Cochrane and Lucy Turnbull
Prop Stylists Charlie Phillips and Louie Waller
Recipe Tester Alexis Winder-Daniel
Proofreader Bianca Bosman
Indexer Beverlee Day

First American Edition, 2023
Published in the United States by DK Publishing
6081 E 82nd Street, Suite 400, Indianapolis, IN 46250

The authorized representative in the EEA is Dorling Kindersley
Verlag GmbH. Arnulfstr. 124, 80636 Munich, Germany

Copyright © 2023 Matt Adlard Ltd.
DK, a Division of Penguin Random House LLC
23 24 25 26 27   10 9 8 7 6 5 4 3 2 1
001–332972–AUG/2023

A catalog record for this book
is available from the Library of Congress.
ISBN 978-0-7440-6490-2

DK books are available at special discounts when purchased in
bulk for sales promotions, premiums, fund-raising, or
educational use. For details, contact: SpecialSales@dk.com

Printed and bound in China

For the curious
www.dk.com

MIX
Paper | Supporting
responsible forestry
FSC™ C018179

This book was made with Forest
Stewardship Council ™ certified
paper – one small step in DK's
commitment to a sustainable future.
For more information go to
www.dk.com/our-green-pledge

FOR SACHA AND RUBEN

Contents

introduction

Introduction

Growing up, it was hard to avoid being around food. My parents ran a Michelin-starred restaurant and living directly above it meant that home and food were always intertwined. Whether it was getting kicked off the computer so Dad could rush to print that evening's menu or eating 'leftovers' from service, life revolved around the bustle of the restaurant. Despite all the years of being exposed to this, the one thing I knew was I never wanted to work in food. I remember vividly being told, "Never become a chef, Matthew!", but here I am, albeit taking a different path, in the industry I never imagined being part of.

Falling into baking wasn't really a conscious thought. I was studying at university, and to stem the boredom of writing essays, I decided to try out a Nigella chocolate-orange cake recipe. Having never baked in my life, and with zero equipment at my disposal, it unsurprisingly didn't turn out well... at all. The cake was inedible, in fact. Most sensible people would probably call it quits after that, but I'm a little stubborn and a perfectionist to say the least, so failure was not an option.

Soon after, I began baking up a storm in our tiny flat, attempting everything from macarons to madeleines. Although cooking was in my blood, my early forays into baking were far from the perfection I had grown up around, with endless hours spent ending with disappointment after another failed trial. But a few years of practice allowed me to hone my skills, and in 2015 I started Topless Baker (which I only slightly wince at in hindsight). Despite laughing at the fact I took my shirt off to bake, looking back, I can see it built my confidence as a presenter and a baker, opening up doors and opportunities that I never thought possible. I remember taking an hour-long bus journey across London every weekend to film videos. I'd take stand mixers, pans, spatulas—virtually my entire kitchen. People looked at me like I was crazy, but I knew somehow the hard work would pay off one day. I was able to grow my social media channels, and connect with an audience of like-minded people, eager to discover the world of baking. As I grew older and my style changed, it was time to put some clothes back on and reintroduce myself, as Matt Adlard. And with that, learning the intricacies of French pastry became my obsession.

Being self-taught and a so-called "influencer"—I've always felt a bit of impostor syndrome, working in an industry surrounded by pastry chefs who have years and years of training. Using the, "Oh, well my dad was a Michelin-starred chef" line was a way of trying to give myself just a smidge of credibility I always felt I lacked. But having written this book, and spent endless hours pulling together all my knowledge, failing more times than you can imagine to get the recipes right, I am so proud of what I've created. I know I can hold my head up and give myself some credit now.

My hope with this book is that you find a baking resource that delivers delicious recipes, time after time. That you'll write notes all over it, fold down the pages, spill cake batter on the cover, and most importantly, grow your confidence in the kitchen, building memories while you bake. Things might go wrong and cakes might burn, but I always like to say it's not the last thing I'll ever eat, then try again!

How To Use This Book

When I began baking, I started with the recipes I love to eat—cookies, white bread, tarts—the simple things! Being self-taught, even tackling these essential recipes was a challenge at first. But through the trials and tribulations resulting in undercooked bread, cracked macarons, burned cookies—the list could go on—I learned a number of lessons along with the fundamentals of baking that became my foundation as I developed my skills.

Once I had mastered these bakes and felt confident, I started to see more and more advanced designs, flavors, and techniques as I scrolled online. My aim was to take these simple recipes I loved, but level them up, be it with a new piping design, an extra layer of flavor—anything to make it more advanced and as close to professional as possible.

The aim of this book is to take you through that process. Each recipe comes as a pair, a Tier 1 recipe and a Tier 2 recipe. The idea is that the Tier 1 recipe will teach you the fundamentals, then when you're ready for Tier 2, you will take a fundamental element from Tier 1, and level it up, creating something worthy of a professional bakery, in your own home.

Now, this advancement from Tier 1 to Tier 2 takes different forms across the book—it could be taking the exact same recipe and adding extra elements to it, as we do in the Chocolate and Mascarpone Cake (page 42) and the Chocolate-Orange Fudge Cake (page 46). In this set, we use the exact same cake recipe for both tiers, but enhance it in the Tier 2 version by adding a ganache filling and a stunning chocolate drip. Or it could be taking a concept and applying it to a more difficult recipe, such as using a pre-ferment to create the Everyday Sandwich Loaf (page 164), then using that same technique to create a more challenging Sea Salt Focaccia (page 166). Although the recipe is different, the fundamental technique of using a pre-ferment is carried through both tiers.

While the aim of Tier 1 is to make these recipes as approachable as possible for all skill levels, so that if you're relatively new to baking you can tackle them, some recipes will vary in difficulty. The Blueberry and Almond Financiers (page 53) are a great way to get started if you're just beginning, but taking on the Hazelnut Praline Mille-Feuille (page 190) if you've never tried puff pastry before, might be a little tougher! However, as you work your way through the book, all the skills and techniques you will learn will build your confidence and knowledge in the kitchen.

My goal is to first encourage you to fail—as ridiculous as that sounds, it will teach you lessons that will be invaluable. Secondly, I want to fill your "recipe locker". For me, my recipe locker is how I build any dessert. Whether it's plucking the dough recipe from the Chia and Black Sesame Shokupan (page 184) and using it for burger buns, or swirling Salted Caramel (page 215) through the Chocolate Chunk Brownies recipe (page 69)—use the recipes as pieces of a jigsaw that you can mix and match how you see fit.

Finally, and most of all, I want you to be able to create professional-looking pastries from the comfort of your home. Too often, pastry is mystified behind secrets and recipes that no one is willing to share. I want everyone to be able to make show-stopping desserts that make your friends and family say, "YOU made that?!"

Ingredients

Butter

Butter is the building block for almost all recipes in this book. It plays such an important role in the flavor and texture of your bakes, so paying attention to the type of butter you use can make a real difference in the final product.

Salted vs. Unsalted: When we are using butter in the recipes, you want to always make sure it is unsalted. Using unsalted butter allows us to control the amount of salt going into a recipe. If we use salted butter, we have no control over this as different brands will use different salt levels, which could result in a bake that is far too salty, or not salty enough.

Fat Percentage: Butter can vary in fat percentages, anywhere from 80% all the way up to 86%. Now, that might seem like a fairly insignificant difference, but actually, that small percentage can have a massive impact on your baked goods. Butter is made up of butterfat, water, and other milk solids. The lower your butterfat content, the more water and milk solids you have going into your baked goods. Just a slight increase in the fat percentage of your butter means you will get a much more buttery taste to bakes, and a more golden color. High–fat percentage butters are also really important if you are working with laminated doughs (croissants, puff pastry, danish, etc.). If you use a butter with a fat percentage under 82%, the butter will have much less flexibility due to the higher water content. This makes the butter stiff, which means it is more likely to "shatter" as you are incorporating it into your dough. As a general rule, look for a "European Style" butter, as these have a minimum fat percentage of 82%. If you have an interest in laminated doughs, look out for professional laminating butter. It can be a little more expensive but is created especially for the likes of croissants and puff pastry, and couldn't be easier to work with.

Chocolate

As you can see from the recipes in the book—I've got a thing for chocolate! When I started baking, however, I never paid much attention to the actual chocolate I was using. But I soon realized that the quality of chocolate you use can play a big role in the taste and outcome of your dessert.

Although it can be one of the more expensive ingredients, good-quality chocolate from brands such as Callebaut, Cacao Barry, or Valrhona not only has a better flavor profile, but contains cocoa butter, which is needed if you want to temper chocolate. Cheaper, grocery store chocolate can often contain oils, which means the chocolate cannot be tempered.

In the recipes I've indicated a cocoa percentage—generally it is a dark chocolate around 70%. You can substitute this for other cocoa percentage chocolates, but just keep in mind that the sugar levels will differ.

Chocolate with a lower cocoa percentage will be sweeter, while chocolate with a higher cocoa percentage will be darker and slightly more bitter.

Yeast

Understanding what yeast to use, how to use it, and what is most effective can be confusing for bakers when they start out. Yeast comes in three main forms: Instant Dry Yeast (IDY), Active Dry Yeast (ADY), and Fresh Yeast, all of which can be used in the recipes.

Active Dry Yeast: You'll often see videos of people adding a little water to yeast, swirling it around, and letting it foam up—this is active dry yeast. As the name suggests, this type of yeast needs activating. To do this is very simple: Take the powdered yeast and add it to a small bowl, with a very small amount of the water or liquid from your recipe, stir it together, and leave it. Within a few minutes, you should see it start to foam up, which means the yeast is alive, active, and ready to be used. The downside to ADY is that it tends to be slightly more perishable, which means that it may not always activate. If you don't see it foaming after a few minutes then it means the yeast is dead and you will need to start again.

Instant Dry Yeast: Sometimes known as "rapid rise" yeast, IDY is a finely granulated powder that, unlike ADY, doesn't need to be activated, which means it can just go straight into the recipe. It tends to be much more reliable that ADY, and unless you're taking a packet that has been sitting in the back of your cupboard for years (!), there's a safe bet it will work. Most recipes in the book use instant dry yeast

Fresh Yeast: Also called "Beer" Yeast in some recipes, this is commonly used in a lot of bakeries. It comes in a crumbly dark block and smells pretty pungent! Unlike dry yeast, which can be stored for months at room temperature, fresh yeast has a limited shelf life, of around 1–2 weeks in the fridge. Fresh yeast can sometimes be a little harder to get hold of, but if you visit a local bakery and ask nicely, they will often bag some up for you to take away. The other downside is due to the limited shelf life it can be hard to tell if that fresh yeast is still active or not, so always ensure you are using it within its shelf life to guarantee your bake's rise.

When it comes to which yeast to use, for me, I have always found fresh yeast to be the most reliable of all three, and something I especially prefer to use when making pre-ferments or laminated dough. But really, it is up to your personal preference and what you find most convenient. If you cannot get hold of fresh yeast, IDY or ADY will absolutely work. ADY and IDY can be substituted 1:1 in any recipe, but keep in mind the IDY can sometimes rise faster so keep an eye on your dough as it is proofing. Fresh yeast, on the other hand, can be substituted for dry yeast 1:2. So use 1g of fresh yeast for every 2g of dry yeast.

Sugar

Granulated/Caster Sugar: As this is a baking book, sugar is a fairly crucial ingredient to discuss. For all of the recipes, I am using caster sugar, which in the UK is a finely ground sugar consisting of much smaller crystals, which dissolve and distribute into recipes much easier than a coarser white sugar. In the US however, granulated sugar is closer in consistency to the UK's caster sugar, therefore no need to go buy the expensive "superfine caster sugar", simply use the granulated sugar from the grocery store. Essentially, when we are incorporating white sugar into a recipe, we want to use a sugar with a very fine granule to avoid any lumps or clumps and ensure that we have a homogeneous mixture once we are done mixing.

Powdered/Icing Sugar: This type of sugar is a much finer powder that can be used for decorative dusting or in cake recipes too. Avoid the online hacks of "making your own"—as commercial powdered (icing) sugar also has anti-caking agents included.

Light Brown Sugar: This is a softer, dark sugar that contains molasses to give it a lovely color and almost caramel-like flavor. This is more hygroscopic than white sugar, so it retains more moisture and therefore is perfect for things like chewy chocolate chip cookies.

Demerara/Turbinado Sugar: While we avoid coarser sugar to bake with, chunkier granulated sugar or turbinado/demerara sugar are perfect decorative sugars as they hold their structure and give you a crunch and sweetness to the tops of things like pies.

Glucose Syrup

Glucose syrup is a sugar substitute used a lot in ice cream, caramel, and glazes. It has a lower sweetness level than regular sugar (about 50% less), helps to prevent crystallization, and gives creams a glossy effect. Although it is usually made from cornstarch/corn flour, I would avoid swapping it for corn syrup in a recipe. Glucose has a lower moisture content, so swapping this out would change the ratios within a recipe.

Gelatin

In this book you will see recipes that call for powdered gelatin. I prefer to use platinum-strength gelatin. There are differing opinions but for me as a general rule, 1 tablespoon of powdered gelatin, equates to 9g, which is the same as 3 sheets of leaf gelatin (any bloom). You can search online for a "gelatin conversion table" if you need to convert different blooms of powdered gelatin.

It is also worth experimenting to see what works best for you, as you may prefer a cream that is slightly thicker or thinner, so you can adjust the level of gelatin to what suits you.

Milk and Cream

In the US, heavy cream (or heavy whipping cream) has a fat percentage of around 36%. Meanwhile, in the UK, double cream has a fat percentage of roughly 32%.

Given these differences, it can be a little confusing to know what to look for and what to use in a recipe. The majority of recipes in this book use heavy/double cream. This has a good level of fat content, meaning that air can be trapped and the cream can be whipped so that it is stable and thick. As a general rule, when buying your cream, take a look at the fat percentage and aim for something between 32–36%.

When it comes to milk, I would recommend always using whole milk with a fat percentage of around 3–3.5%.

Ground Almonds

Ground almonds are seen in a lot of French baking—they bring moisture and "butteriness" to baked goods. They often go by a few names—ground almonds, almond meal, almond flour, and almond powder—which can add to the confusion of which one to use.

Essentially, ground almonds are skinned, blanched almonds that have been blended into a relatively fine powder. Because the skin has been removed, they are light in color. In contrast, almond meal is the same thing, but typically the skin of the almond hasn't been removed. Really, this makes little difference to the outcome of the recipes, so they can be substituted 1:1. Almond flour and almond powder can also fall into either of these categories, so if in doubt, simply look at the texture, and the color. You are looking for a relatively fine texture ideally with no color, but if it is slightly darker, that will work perfectly too.

Eggs

In all the recipes you will see eggs by weight—the reason I have done this is that eggs vary in size, from small to extra large, and these sizes also differ by country. Different sized eggs have different ratios of yolk and white, which has a knock on effect on the recipe. By using the weight of the egg in a recipe, it means you can make the recipes as consistent as possible, regardless of the size of eggs available. So, to weigh the eggs for a recipe, weigh the bowl you'll be using on the scale and then tare it, crack the eggs into the bowl, whisk them very thoroughly to make sure there are no thick streaks of egg white, then weigh the required amount. To get an idea of exactly how much one egg weighs, I would recommend taking the eggs you usually buy, cracking one into a bowl, and reading the weight. Then separate the yolk and whites and weigh these as well. From there, you have an idea on exactly how many eggs you will need for the recipe. As a guide, one large egg (without the shell) tends to be around 60g, with the yolk between 18–20g and the white between 40–42g. All the eggs in the recipes are kept at room temperature, but if you have them in the fridge and need to bring them up to temperature quickly, take the whole egg in the shell, and place it in a bowl of warm water just for a couple of minutes before cracking and weighing it.

Flour

Flour plays a key role in baking—binding ingredients and helping to create structure. Choosing the right type of flour to use can have a big impact on the final outcome of a baked good, and the amount of gluten you are aiming to develop.

Different types of flour have different levels of protein, and protein levels are important to take note of because protein helps to develop gluten. This means, a flour with a higher protein level will allow you to create more gluten, giving the final product more strength. This works great for something like bread, but for a cake, which you want to be light and fluffy... not so much!

Bread Flour/White Bread Flour: Bread flour is designed—well as it says—for bread! This flour typically has a much higher protein content, around 11–13%, which means you can develop more gluten in your dough, which is needed to give bread strength and help it to rise. Because of the higher gluten development, it results in a chewier texture and airy crumb, perfect for breads and yeasted doughs. If a recipe calls for bread flour, I would highly recommend using it and not substituting it for an alternative.

Pastry/Cake Flour: On the opposite end of the spectrum is pastry or cake flour, a much softer flour with a protein content of 7–9%. The lower protein content is ideal for things such as light sponges or sweet pastry. I had never used it until a few years ago and immediately noticed the difference it made, especially when making cakes. This can easily be substituted for all-purpose/plain flour, which will result in a slightly tougher product but nothing too noticeable. Avoid the DIY cake flours, as these can't miraculously lower the protein content of your flour!

All-Purpose/Plain Flour: More of an all-rounder, all-purpose flour has a protein level of 10–12%, meaning it sits on the edge of both cake and bread flour. This is a versatile flour that can be used in cakes and pastry but also, things such as donuts or brioche.

Self-Rising/Self-Raising Flour: With a protein content of 8–11%, this is closer to a pastry/all-purpose blend, but with baking powder, and sometimes salt, also included. The lower protein content means it results in a softer baked good that doesn't require any additional leavening agents.

Tools & Equipment

After years and years of baking, I don't think there isn't a mold, tool, or tray that hasn't passed through my kitchen at one point! Having so many gadgets is great, but I wanted to make sure that all the recipes in the book were made with equipment that hopefully you have in the house, or at least is readily available online for you. Where I have used a certain pan or mold, I have tried my best to use it in other recipes, so that it has more than one use and you can recreate as many of the recipes as possible.

I'm going to take for granted your kitchen is teaming with bowls, spatulas, and whisks, so I won't list some of the more obvious tools, but the ones I think are a huge help to have when it comes to baking.

Digital Scales and Micro Scales

In this book, you will see everything is weighed using the metric system—grams. Now, there is a big debate about whether metric or imperial is the best for baking and I'll avoid trying to create too much of a stir, while giving you my opinion. Baking is a science, and that means, the balance of every ingredient plays a crucial role in the outcome. Not quite enough eggs, and your choux will be flat. Too much baking powder, and your cake will explode. This means that being as precise as possible will give you consistent bakes, time after time. Using cups, however, can lead to quite a lot of inconsistencies due to the way that people scoop flour or how they level a cup. Should you pack the flour down? Or gently level it with a knife? All these nuances lead to inaccuracies, which ultimately means your bakes will never be consistent. And so, we have grams. Regardless of where you are in the world, 100g of flour is 100g of flour. So in this book, everything is weighed—liquid, dry goods, zest—*everything*!

This brings me to the first piece of equipment that is a must—a set of digital scales. These are cheap and cheerful and can be picked up easily online. But I promise, if you've never used them before, they will instantly improve your baking. It takes all the guesswork out and means that when you nail a recipe, you can do it time and time again!

If you want to go a little further, it is also worth getting micro scales. These typically measure ingredients in 0.1g intervals—very precise. Having such a high level of accuracy doesn't really matter when you are measuring flour or sugar, but when you are using ice cream stabilizers, or gelatin for example, where you only need a very small amount—just a few grams over or under can really affect the outcome of your dessert.

Instant Read Thermometers

In certain recipes, such as macarons or ice cream, hitting specific temperatures during the baking process is crucial to achieving the correct outcome. A cheap instant read thermometer can be invaluable and will give you a quick, accurate reading. I would recommend using an instant read thermometer with a metal probe as opposed to an infrared gun.

Oven Thermometer

While this might not be necessary if you have a nice new oven—often the temperature you set your oven to, and the actual internal temperature can differ. As a result of this discrepancy, it can throw off your timings and the results of a certain bake. An oven thermometer can give you an accurate reading inside the oven and allow you to adjust the temperature accordingly.

Digital Calipers

Put it under the "nice to have" category, but this is something that I use every day! A digital caliper is an electronic precision tool that gives you highly accurate measurement readings. Throughout the book you will see a lot of detailed measurements for the width of molds or the thickness of dough. Calipers are cheap and easily available and allow you to quickly and accurately measure items which, in turn, leads to a more consistent product when you can ensure the width or thickness is the same every time.

Stand Mixer

My favorite appliance and one that not only looks sleek in the kitchen, but opens up a world of bakes that would otherwise be incredibly laborious and challenging. While making a silky meringue or buttery brioche by hand is possible, a stand mixer offers you a consistent, efficient, and time-saving option, and takes the hard work out of the equation.

A hand mixer is not out of the question for mixing things like cookie dough—but when it comes to kneading dough or aerating a cake batter, a stand mixer will always deliver a better final product.

If you like to work with bread doughs or are looking to handle big batches of baked goods, then I would definitely recommend a larger mixer (7.2 quart/6.8 liter) with a more powerful motor. Meanwhile, a standard size (5.1 quart/4.8 liter) is perfect when making meringues, macarons, or cakes—when you might be working with smaller quantities but still need the power of the motor to do the work for you.

Hand Blender

A good hand blender allows you to easily emulsify ingredients that otherwise may be more difficult to do by hand. Hand blenders can vary greatly in price, however, if you want to invest, a Bamix hand blender is really one of the best when it comes to pastry. The design of the head and blades means that very little air is incorporated as you blend, meaning you are able to achieve bubble-free mirror glazes and ganaches. Although air bubbles are just an aesthetic, being able to eliminate them can elevate the presentation of your bakes.

Perforated Tart Rings and Mats

Perforated tart rings are metal baking rings with small holes all around the outside and no base. The purpose of all these little holes is to allow maximum airflow while the tart bakes and to prevent any steam from building up, which results in a more even bake. Combining these with a perforated baking mat, and a perforated tray (which also have lots of little holes) means you do not need to blind-bake pastry. Because of the airflow, there is no need to add baking paper and baking beans/rice, which is usually used to prevent the pastry from puffing up as it bakes.

Although they can be slightly more expensive, they will take your pastry to the next level, and give you a much more professional, clean finish to your tarts.

So that you don't have too many sets of rings, in the book, I generally use individual perforated tart rings that are 3 × 0.75 inches (7.62 × 1.91cm). You can use any size perforated tart ring you prefer, however, keep in mind any adjustments you might need to make to the recipe quantities.

Ovens: Conventional vs. Convection

While an oven might seem to be an obvious appliance you will need—there are different types of oven and multiple settings that can change the way temperature is distributed. When I started baking, I watched a video where someone said not to use the convection/fan-assisted setting on ovens because the force of the air from the fan could blow over your soufflé or make your macarons lopsided! Now, while I'm not quite sure that is true... it still scares me to this day to imagine working so hard, only to see my soufflé get blown over as it bakes!

Convection ovens evenly distribute heat throughout an oven by using the fan at the back to circulate the hot air. This means there are fewer cold spots, and it generally is said to cook things more evenly. While these seem like obvious reasons to only use a convection oven to bake, the hot air flow and efficient heat distribution can lead to a drier atmosphere in the oven (so less moisture in your bakes) and can cause things to bake much faster. This means cakes could be cooked on the outside but still raw in the center, leading to a dry overcooked cake once the center finally bakes.

A conventional oven on the other hand generally has two heating elements, one at the top and one at the bottom, radiating a stationary heat from both sides. While this can result in some cold spots in the oven, generally it is said to be better for baking due to the atmosphere in the oven and the fact that it doesn't cook items as quickly.

Therefore, in this book, all temperatures and timings refer to a conventional oven setting (no fan). If you do have a convection oven, then you will need to lower the temperature of the oven by roughly 25°F/15°C for each recipe. While this might sound obvious, always keep an eye on your bakes. Ovens can vary so greatly in performance and heat distribution that you need to use the recipe combined with your instincts as to when you think something is done. If a recipe says to bake for 25 minutes, always have a look after 15 minutes and keep checking it from then on, just to see the progress and look for signs that it might be ready. It might take a few burned cakes or raw soufflés to dial in your oven and really see how it behaves!

CHAPTER 2

techniques

Pastry

Making pastry is one of my favorite processes. Growing up and watching my dad make it so effortlessly for his lemon tart, I always assumed it was easy. Once I started baking, I had endless troubles with the pastry cracking, shrinking, or just not really tasting very good at all. So I set out to make a recipe using a versatile technique that solves these issues.

Throughout the book you will see pastry featured across a number of recipes, and rather than giving you a short explanation that lacked detail, I wanted to give you all the information up front, so that you would be better prepared to tackle the recipes.

Below I have created one base recipe that has been adapted for vanilla, lemon, or chocolate pastry dough. The versatility of it means you can adapt it to your preferences—whether you want to create a chocolate-orange pastry or a cardamom-vanilla one. Experiment with these base flavors and see what you end up with! The step-by-step guide will take you through how to blind-bake the pastry, so you'll be ready to add your filling. **Keep an eye on the recipe you are using though, as not all the recipes in the book will need you to blind bake the pastry first.**

In this book we generally use a fluted tart ring with a removable base in the Tier 1 recipes, while the Tier 2 recipes use perforated rings. I dive into perforated rings in more detail in the equipment section (page 25), but they are a game changer and will give you a professional finish to any pastry you make.

VANILLA	LEMON	CHOCOLATE
70g powdered/icing sugar	70g powdered/icing sugar	70g powdered/icing sugar
100g unsalted butter, cold and cubed	100g unsalted butter, cold and cubed	100g unsalted butter, cold and cubed
½ tsp vanilla bean paste	2g lemon zest	20g cocoa powder
50g egg yolks	50g egg yolks	50g egg yolks
200g all-purpose/plain flour, plus a pinch of sea salt	200g all-purpose/plain flour, plus a pinch of sea salt	180g all-purpose/plain flour, plus a pinch of sea salt

EGG WASH	COCOA EGG WASH
40g egg yolks	40g egg yolks, plus 5g cocoa powder
10g heavy/double cream	10g heavy/double cream

Removable Base Tart Pan/Tin

The technique below is to line a 9-inch (23cm) fluted tart pan/tin with a removable base.

1. To make the pastry, into the bowl of a stand mixer fitted with the paddle attachment, sift in the sugar. Add the butter and your flavoring—vanilla, lemon, or cocoa powder.

2. Beat for 2–3 minutes, or until the mixture forms a smooth paste, pausing to scrape down the sides as needed.

3. Add in the egg yolks, scrape down the sides and beat for 30 seconds, or until incorporated.

4. Scrape down the bowl once again to ensure no butter is stuck to the sides. Add the flour and salt and mix on low speed for about 20–30 seconds, or until the mixture pulls together into a dough.

5. Remove the dough from the bowl and gently work it into a disk shape. Wrap the dough in plastic wrap/cling film and refrigerate for 30 minutes.

6. Take the dough out of the fridge and gently squeeze it, using your hands to test the firmness. You want the dough to be slightly pliable but still cold. If the dough is too soft it will get sticky as you roll, but if it is too cold it will crack. It might need a minute or two at room temperature to get it to the right consistency.

7. Lightly flour the dough and your rolling pin and, working quickly, roll the dough into a rough circle until the pastry is relatively thin, about 0.15–0.2 inches (0.4mm–0.5mm) thick. Lift the dough up occasionally and lightly flour underneath to prevent it from sticking. If the dough is tearing or feels too warm, place it on a baking tray and refrigerate for 10–15 minutes, then try again.

8. Place your rolling pin at the top of the circle and fold the top edge of the dough over the rolling pin. Pull the rolling pin back towards you, which will wrap the dough around the rolling pin.

9. Starting at the bottom edge of your fluted tart pan, carefully unroll the dough from the rolling pin, covering the entire pan.

10. Use your fingers to gently press the dough into the edges of the fluted indents. If the dough is tearing, simply take any excess pastry and patch the holes.

11. Take the rolling pin, and, pressing firmly against the top of the pan, roll it over the entire pan to trim away the excess dough. Place the pan on a tray and pop it into the freezer for 30 minutes. Preheat your oven to 355°F/180°C.

12. Cut a large circle of parchment paper, and scrunch this up a few times so that it is flexible. Remove the tray from the freezer and use a fork to poke holes evenly across the base of the pastry.

13. Place the parchment paper on the inside of the pastry and press it into the edges. Pour your baking beans or rice into the base and spread them out. Place the tray with the pan on in the oven and bake for 25 minutes.

14. After 25 minutes, remove the tray from the oven and carefully lift out the parchment paper with the baking beans on. Return the tray to the oven and continue to bake until the pastry is an even golden color—about 5–10 minutes.

15. Remove the tray from the oven and allow the pastry to cool for 10 minutes.

16. Mix together the ingredients for the egg wash. If you are making the cocoa egg wash, really thoroughly mix it to make sure the cocoa powder is incorporated. Don't use the regular egg wash or you will get yellow streaks on your tart shell!

17. Using a pastry brush, lightly egg wash the inside of the tart shell. Place it onto the tray and back into the oven for 5–7 minutes, or until the egg wash has completely set and the pastry is golden.

18. Remove the tart from the oven, allowing it to cool slightly. It is now ready to add your filling. It is important to leave the tart shell in the pan, especially when adding a very liquid-y filling (like the one in My Dad's Lemon Tart, page 82). This provides extra support and prevents the pastry from breaking or bending.

Note: If you are using the chocolate pastry recipe, it is harder to tell when the pastry is done as you cannot see the color changing, so follow these timings, but keep a close eye on it to ensure it doesn't burn.

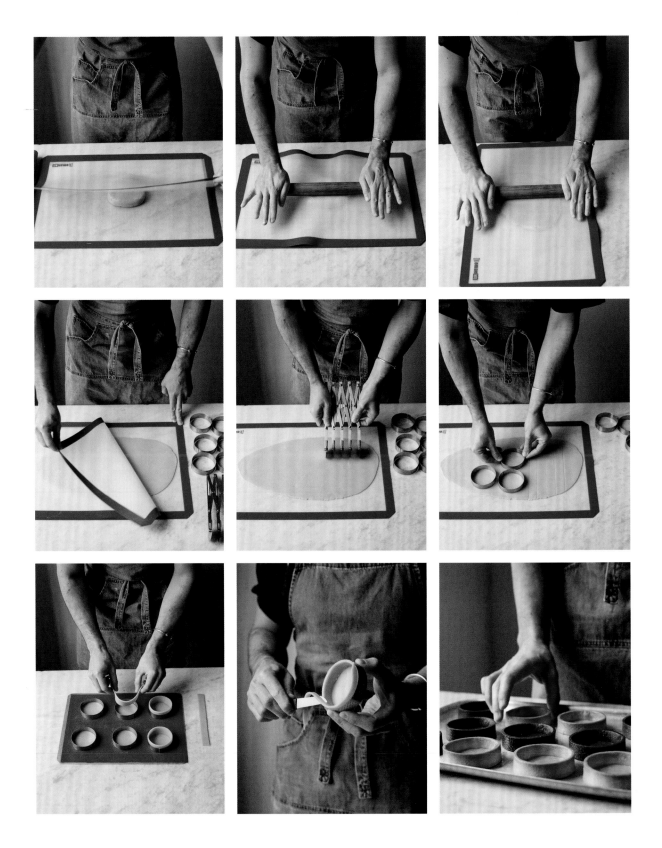

Perforated Tart Rings

The technique below is for lining six 3 × 0.8-inch (7.6 2cm) perforated tart rings. The same technique applies when using larger tart rings, but any excess dough may need to be re-rolled and chilled in order to have enough dough to fit all the rings.

1. To make the pastry, into the bowl of a stand mixer fitted with the paddle attachment, sift in the sugar. Add the butter and your flavoring.

2. Beat for 2–3 minutes, or until the mixture forms a smooth paste, scraping down the sides as needed.

3. Add in the egg yolks, scrape down the sides, and beat for 30 seconds, or until incorporated.

4. Scrape down the bowl once again. Add the flour and salt and mix on low speed for 20–30 seconds, or until the mixture pulls together into a dough.

5. Squeeze the mixture to form a rough ball. Place the dough onto a silicone mat. Place a second silicone mat on top and roll the mixture into a rough rectangle, getting it around 0.15–0.2 inch (4mm–5mm) thick. If you don't have silicone mats you use parchment paper, but it will be more difficult. Place it in the freezer for 20 minutes.

6. While the dough is chilling, take the perforated tart rings and very lightly grease the insides with soft butter. This helps to prevent the dough from sticking to the ring.

7. Remove the dough from the freezer and, working quickly, peel the top silicone mat off of the dough. Press 4 tart rings firmly into the dough, lift them up, and transfer them to a perforated tray lined with a perforated baking mat. The dough should be cold enough that it attaches to the ring as you lift it up. Place the tray in the fridge while you cut the walls.

8. With the remaining dough, use a ruler and a sharp knife to cut 4 strips of dough each measuring 9.6 × 0.9 inches (24.4 × 2.3cm). These measurements seem quite precise, but this will ensure the dough fits perfectly into the tart rings. If they feel too warm to lift up, freeze them for 5 minutes.

Note: If you are using a perforated tart ring that is bigger, you will need to increase the length of the strips to fit the ring.

9. Remove the baking tray with the tart bases from the fridge and remove one strip of dough.

10. Working quickly, take the strip of dough and place it inside a tart ring. Use your fingers to gently press together this strip of dough, against the base of the tart. The idea is to slightly push down the wall of dough so that it meets the dough on the base of the tart shell and there are no gaps. If at any point you feel the dough is too warm or is tearing, place everything back in the freezer for 10 minutes.

11. Repeat this with the remaining rings. Squeeze together the remaining scraps of dough, and repeat the process, rolling the dough and chilling it, so that you can create the final 2 tart shells.

12. Once you have lined all the tart shells, avoid trying to move them in case the dough tears. Chill the tray for 15 minutes and preheat your oven to 345°F/175°C.

13. Remove the shells from the freezer and holding a knife perpendicular to the tart shell, trim off the excess pastry hanging over the tart ring so that the pastry is flush.

14. Place the tart shells in the oven, and bake for 15 minutes, or until they are lightly golden on the base. While they bake, thoroughly whisk together the ingredients for the egg wash.

15. Remove the tarts from the oven and allow them to cool for 5 minutes. The pastry should have retracted slightly from the ring mold, and you should be able to lift it easily.

16. Lift the shells up and using a pastry brush, apply an even egg wash all over the tart. Place them back on the tray and bake for a further 5–8 minutes, or until the pastry is a golden color.

Tempering Chocolate

While it may be one of the most intimidating techniques in pastry for a home baker, in simple terms, tempering chocolate is the processing of heating and cooling to specific temperature parameters.

The aim of heating and cooling chocolate this way is to create beta crystals, which, when formed, create a stable chocolate with a smooth, shiny finish, and a nice snap—the exact properties you need to make things such as bonbons or chocolate decorations.

When it comes to tempering you need to use good-quality chocolate (see page 14) that contains cocoa butter. The beta crystals I mentioned above that we need to form shiny tempered chocolate, are only present in cocoa butter, making it a critical ingredient. Chocolate that is ideal for tempering usually comes in a droplet or callet form. These resemble giant chocolate chips, and they're perfect for tempering due to their consistency and size. If you don't have these, chop your chocolate into small, relatively even pieces.

It's worth trying out all of the tempering methods to see what works best for you, and what you feel most comfortable and confident in using. It will get a bit messy, but once you've mastered it, it is a skill that will become like second nature.

One thing to note, and something that took me a really long time to realize, is that the amount of chocolate you use can determine how hard you make the tempering process for yourself. Imagine boiling water—if you boil a tiny cup of water, it only takes a very short amount of time, versus boiling a large pot of water, which takes several minutes. Now, apply that same theory to tempering, remembering that you also need to hit precise temperatures as you heat and cool the chocolate.

If you need to temper a tiny amount of chocolate, it is extremely difficult to hit the precise temperatures because of how quickly it will melt and heat up. This means that realistically you are more than likely to overheat it, thus making it impossible to then temper. Meanwhile, if you are melting a larger batch of chocolate, it will take a lot longer for that amount to reach those temperatures, and you will have much more time and control, to ensure that you hit the exact temperature guides. Therefore, I always liked to work with a minimum of around 400g of chocolate to temper. This might be slightly more than you need, and takes a little bit longer to temper, but overall makes the experience a lot less stressful! And once you're done with the tempered chocolate, you can pour it onto a tray, let it set, then use it to temper another time.

Different chocolate brands have different "temperature curves" in order to create tempered chocolate. If you're unsure, the packaging of any high-quality chocolate should give these details. Here are general guidelines:

DARK CHOCOLATE

1. Melt to: 113–122°F/45–50°C

2. Cool to: 84°F/29°C

3. Working Temperature: 84–93°F/29–34°C

MILK CHOCOLATE

1. Melt to: 113–122°F/45–50°C

2. Cool to: 82°F/28°C

3. Working Temperature: 82–88°F/28–31.5°C

WHITE CHOCOLATE

1. Heat to: 113–122°F/45–50°C

2. Cool to: 82°F/28°C

3. Working Temperature: 82–88°F/28–31.5°C

In the methods below I will use dark chocolate, but the same technique applies for all chocolate types—simply adjust the temperatures according to what you are using.

Seeding

The process of seeding involves melting chocolate over low heat, then adding stable beta crystals (i.e unmelted chocolate) in order to create the crystallization process that results in tempered chocolate. This process is one of the most common, but can be time consuming, especially with larger quantities of chocolate.

1. Place 335g of dark chocolate into a medium bowl (ideally a heatproof plastic bowl). Place it over a medium saucepan of very gently simmering water, ensuring the water doesn't touch the bowl. Place the heat on low.

2. Stir constantly with a rubber spatula, ensuring your digital thermometer is always in the chocolate, reading the temperature.

3. Once the chocolate reaches 113°F/45°C, immediately remove the bowl from the heat.

4. Place the bowl onto a kitchen/tea towel and then tip in 20% of the original weight of chocolate—65g.

5. Stir the mixture **constantly**, ensuring you scrape down the sides of the bowl and regularly check the temperature with your digital thermometer. Continue to stir the chocolate until the temperature has dropped to 84°F/29°C.

Note: Once you become more confident, you can actually cool the chocolate over a bowl of cold water to speed things up. I wouldn't recommend this with your first few attempts as chocolate and water are a bad combination and if you spill any water in the chocolate it will be a disaster!

6. At this point your chocolate is in temper and ready to use.

7. If you are not quite ready to use your chocolate, stir it occasionally and use a heat gun or hair dryer maintain that working temperature. The chocolate will begin to thicken the longer you wait, in which case you may want to increase the temperature to anywhere up to 93°F/34°C. This will make it more fluid and easier to work with. Do not go above this temperature or your chocolate will be out of temper.

Tabling

Tabling is a great tempering process as it is much quicker than seeding, especially if you are tempering a large quantity of chocolate. The method I use below is cheating a little bit as we are going to "table" the chocolate onto a sheet of plastic wrap/cling film. It's not as fancy as the expert chocolatiers you see scraping it all over the table, but it saves your kitchen from getting covered in chocolate!

Ensure you have a surface covered with a very large sheet (or several sheets) of plastic wrap before you start (sticking it down with a little bit of oil can help!), and a kitchen/tea towel at the ready.

1. Place 400g of dark chocolate into a medium bowl (ideally a heatproof plastic bowl). Place it over a medium saucepan of very gently simmering water. Make sure the heat is on low.

2. Stir constantly with a rubber spatula, ensuring your digital thermometer is always in the chocolate, reading the temperature.

3. Once the chocolate reaches 113°F/45°C, immediately remove the bowl from the heat.

4. Once at temperature, thoroughly dry the bottom of the bowl to prevent any water dripping into the chocolate, and pour ⅔ of the chocolate onto the cling film. Set the bowl to one side.

5. Use a rubber spatula to spread the chocolate out, providing **constant** movement—spreading the chocolate out, then scooping it all together, spreading it out etc.

6. Use the spatula to create a pool of chocolate, then insert your digital thermometer to read the temperature. Once at 80.5°F/27°C, carefully roll the plastic wrap up into a log, lift it up, snip off the end with a pair of scissors, and squeeze the cooled chocolate into the original bowl of melted chocolate that you set to the side.

7. Immediately stir it together and check the temperature. If it is a little below the working temperature of 84–93°F/29–34°C, then you can gently heat it on the pan of simmering water or use a heat gun/hair dryer to warm it. Once you are at the working temperature, your chocolate is in temper.

Microwave

Because of the time it takes with both the seeding and the tabling method, the microwave is often one of the most preferred techniques to temper chocolate. Just make sure you don't overheat it!

1. Place 400g of dark chocolate into a heatproof, microwave-safe bowl (ideally not glass) and place it in the microwave, on high heat for 30 seconds. Stir the mixture thoroughly, (it might not have melted much at all) and place it back in for another 30 seconds.

2. Stir the chocolate mixture again, scraping off and incorporating any chocolate that sticks to the spatula, and keep heating it at 10–15 second intervals, stirring inbetween each one.

3. Once the chocolate has melted and has a good fluidity, but there are still a few lumps of chocolate, stop heating it, and use the spatula to constantly stir the chocolate until those pieces of chocolate have completely melted.

4. At this point, read the temperature of your chocolate, which should be at a good working temperature, between 84–93°F (29–34°C).

5. If the chocolate is too warm, continue to stir it until it cools down. If it is too cold, use a heat gun or a hair dryer to gently heat it up.

Kneading Dough

While kneading dough is made simple with stand mixers these days, learning to knead dough by hand is an important technique. Using your hands to feel the dough and how the structure and texture change as you knead it, helps to give you a much better understanding of what exactly you're looking for.

It can be a messy process and one that might cause you to second guess yourself, but with time and some patience, you will end up with a perfectly smooth dough.

Without getting too technical, the aim of kneading is to develop the proteins within the flour to form strands of gluten. As you develop the gluten, the dough will gradually become more elastic and change from a rough consistency to a smooth dough. Doing this by hand can take around 10 minutes if you are just starting out, but as you gain more confidence and experience, you will be able to speed this process up.

There are a number of different techniques to knead dough by hand, but it really comes down to simply stretching and folding the dough, over and over. I prefer to use the "push and pull" method (a name I've just made up!).

For this example, I will use the dough recipe from the Tangzhong Garlic Dough Balls (page 180).

1. Start by adding the dry ingredients for your dough into a large mixing bowl. Swirl them around to combine them with your hand, then pour over the wet ingredients. Use your hands again to mix, until there are no dry bits remaining in the bowl.

2. Very lightly flour your work surface and dump the shaggy dough out of the bowl and shape it into a rough circle.

3. With the fingertips of your non-dominant hand, grip the back of the dough ball, then with the heel of your dominant hand, press the dough away from you, stretching it out. At this point, the dough will will likely tear. That is totally normal as we haven't developed any gluten and elasticity yet.

4. Take the edge of the dough furthest from you, and flip it back on itself, almost folding the dough in half. Lift up the dough with both hands, rotate it 90°, and place it back down. Now, repeat this stretching and folding motion. Do this over and over for 5–10 minutes until you have a smooth dough.

5. When you start kneading, you might notice the dough is sticking to you and you may be tempted to add a lot of flour to avoid this. By adding more flour, you are actually changing the ratios in the recipe, which could affect the outcome of the dough. So, if you feel it is getting too sticky, you can very lightly wet your hands and carry on. This sounds counterintuitive but it helps to repel the dough. A great piece of equipment to use is a bench scraper. A metal bench scraper can help you to more easily maneuver the dough throughout the process, as well as pick up any little scraps that may be stuck.

6. As you continue to knead, you will notice the dough will become a lot smoother, and much easier to stretch. To check if the dough is done, you need to see if you have developed enough gluten, and you can do this by performing a "window pane test."

7. Tear off a small chunk of dough, and with your hands, gently stretch the dough until you create a film of dough that is thin enough to see through. If the dough tears as you are stretching it, you have not developed enough gluten and you need to carry on working the dough. But, if you are able to stretch the dough easily and create the windowpane, your dough is ready and you can proof it.

8. To finish the dough, cup both hands on the underside of the dough ball and gently rotate it in a circular motion on the work surface. This should build some tension and leave you with a smooth ball. Transfer the dough into a lightly oiled bowl, cover it with plastic wrap/cling film, and proof it.

CHAPTER 3

cakes

Chocolate and Mascarpone Travel Cake

MAKES 1 LOAF CAKE

Soft butter, for greasing

175g hot coffee or water

50g cocoa powder, plus more
for dusting

175g buttermilk

110g neutral/vegetable oil

95g eggs

185g cake/pastry flour (or
all-purpose/plain flour)

290g granulated/caster sugar

14g baking soda

3g sea salt

½ batch Vanilla Mascarpone
Cream (Page 218)

SPECIAL EQUIPMENT

2lb (900g) loaf pan/tin

Stand mixer, with the
whisk attachment

Piping bag with a St. Honoré
nozzle (or any nozzle you
prefer)

I've always found that other chocolate cake recipes weren't quite chocolaty enough, but the secret is blooming the cocoa powder in hot coffee or water. This cake gets better with time, so I always chill it in the fridge for 2–3 days.

1. Preheat the oven to 345°F/175°C, and lightly grease the inside of a 2-pound (900g) loaf pan with butter. Add in a tablespoon of cocoa powder and shake around to coat. Tap out any excess and set the pan to one side.

2. Add the hot coffee and cocoa powder to a medium saucepan set over medium heat and whisk until it reaches a gentle simmer. Set aside and allow it to cool for 10–15 minutes.

3. Into a tall measuring jug/cup, add the buttermilk, oil, and eggs. Whisk to combine, but don't worry if it looks like it hasn't fully combined.

4. Into a large mixing bowl, sift in the flour, sugar, baking soda, and salt. Whisk to combine.

5. Pour the buttermilk mixture into the dry ingredients and whisk, ensuring to scrape the bottom of the bowl to incorporate any dry bits.

6. Slowly pour in the cooled cocoa mixture, whisking until you have a smooth batter. It will be slightly thin in consistency.

7. Pour the mixture into your lined pan, then place it in the oven. Bake for 50–60 minutes, or until a skewer inserted comes out clean.

8. Remove the cake from the oven and allow it to cool for a few minutes in the pan before carefully flipping it out onto a wire rack.

9. Immediately wrap the cake in the plastic wrap/cling film and place it in the fridge with the smooth bottom of the cake, facing up. Let it chill overnight. You can leave this in the fridge for a few days if need be.

10. Prepare ½ a batch of the Vanilla Mascarpone Cream and allow this to chill overnight too.

11. Remove the chilled cake from the fridge and dust ¾ of the top of the cake with a light layer of cocoa powder.

12. Add the Vanilla Mascarpone Cream to the bowl of a stand mixer fitted with the whisk attachment and whisk on medium speed until you have a medium-stiff peak.

13. Add the mixture into a piping bag fitted with a St. Honoré nozzle and then pipe a thin zigzag down the side of the cake not coated with cocoa powder. Allow the cake to come to room temperature before serving.

Chocolate-Orange Fudge Cake

MAKES 1 CAKE

FOR THE CAKE

470g water

125g cocoa powder, plus 3 tbsp for dusting

780g sugar

38g baking soda

490g cake/pastry flour (or all-purpose/plain flour)

5g orange zest

470g buttermilk

245g eggs

295g neutral/vegetable oil

FOR THE GANACHE

465g dark chocolate, 70% cocoa solids

465g heavy/double cream

35g light brown sugar

35g glucose syrup

60g unsalted butter

175g crème fraîche

FOR THE DRIP

100g dark chocolate, 70% cocoa solids

60g unsalted butter

Chocolate curls, to decorate

A chocolate-orange cake was the first recipe I ever tried to bake, and it was a disaster. I still have the photo to remind me! This cake, however, is a showstopper. We are using the cake recipe from Tier 1 (page 42), but adding a ganache filling and using a scalloped cake scraper to create a professional bakery-style edge.

1. Preheat your oven to 345°F/175°C.

2. Add the water and cocoa powder to a medium saucepan. Place it over a medium heat and whisk the mixture until it reaches a gentle simmer and the cocoa powder has completely dissolved. Turn off the heat and let it cool for 10 minutes.

3. Meanwhile, add the sugar, baking soda, flour, and orange zest to a large bowl. Whisk this together to ensure everything is evenly combined.

4. Add the buttermilk, eggs, and oil to a separate mixing bowl. Whisk to combine, then pour the mixture into the bowl of dry ingredients.

5. Pour in the cooled cocoa mixture and whisk constantly until it has been completely incorporated and there are no streaks. The batter will be quite thin, but don't panic.

6. Grease the bottom and sides of three 3 × 9-inch (7.5 × 23 cm) cake pans and then place a circle of parchment paper on the bottom. Add a tablespoon of cocoa powder into each pan and shake it around to coat the edges. Tip out any excess.

7. Pour the cake batter into the pans, weighing 900g of batter per pan.

8. Place the cakes into the preheated oven and bake for around 45 minutes, or until a skewer comes out clean.

9. Once the cakes have baked, let them cool for 5 minutes, and then very carefully flip them onto a wire rack to cool. The cakes are quite soft, therefore will be fragile, so be as careful as possible.

10. Let the cakes cool for 10 minutes on a wire rack, then wrap them in plastic wrap/cling film and refrigerate them for at least 6 hours.

11. For the ganache, start by adding your chocolate into a medium bowl and place it over a pan of gently simmering water. Keep stirring this until it has completely melted.

12. Meanwhile, add the cream, brown sugar, glucose, and butter to a medium saucepan. Place this over medium heat until it is steamy, and the butter has completely melted. Make sure to stir occasionally.

3× 3 × 9-inch (7.5 × 23 cm)
cake pans/tins

Hand blender

Rotating cake stand with a
cake board

Offset spatula

Straight and scalloped edge
scrapers

Hair dryer or heat gun

Instant read thermometer

NOTE: As you work with the ganache it may thicken too much as it cools—simply use a hair dryer or a heat gun and carefully heat the ganache while stirring until the consistency is looser and it is smooth and glossy again.

13. Once the cream is hot, remove the chocolate from the heat, and with a spatula, stir the chocolate constantly in small circular motions in the center, while slowly pouring in the hot cream.

14. Keep stirring the mixture until all the cream has been incorporated into the chocolate. At this point it may look slightly grainy, but don't panic.

15. Add in the crème fraîche, and then use a hand blender to blend it until smooth. Using a hand blender will allow the mixture to completely emulsify, which will result in a smooth, glossy ganache.

16. Cover the surface with plastic wrap/cling film and leave it at room temperature for 2–3 hours, or until it has thickened to a consistency that resembles buttercream. You will need to stir it occasionally to prevent any lumps forming around the outside.

17. Once the ganache is ready, remove your chilled cake layers from the fridge.

18. Place your first cake layer onto a cake board, on a rotating cake stand. Add a dollop of the ganache and then use an offset spatula to smooth it out.

19. Add the second layer of cake and add another even coating of the ganache. Finally top it with the final cake layer.

20. Take a dollop of the ganache and spread this over the top of the cake and around the edges. Use a tall straight edge scraper to smooth the ganache, and create an even crumb coat around the outside. Use a hair dryer or heat gun as needed to heat and smooth any ganache that may have set.

21. Once you have an even crumb coat, refrigerate for 20 minutes.

22. When the cake has chilled, spread the remaining ganache over the cake, trying to keep the top as smooth as possible while leaving the outside relatively rough. Then gently heat a scalloped cake scraper and carefully run this around the outside of the cake to create the design. Fill in any gaps with extra ganache and repeat this scraping process. Place the cake back in the fridge for 20 minutes.

23. To make the drip, add the chocolate and butter to a small bowl and melt it over a pan of gently simmering water. Once melted, cool to 90°F/32°C.

24. Once the drip is at temperature, remove the cake from the fridge and pour the glaze onto the middle of the cake. Working quickly, use an offset spatula to spread it to the edges until it drips down the side.

25. Finish the cake with chocolate curls around the top. Allow it to come to room temperature before serving.

Lemon and Poppy Seed Tray Bake

MAKES 1 CAKE

FOR THE CAKE

Unsalted butter, for greasing

275g eggs

275g powdered/icing sugar

6g lemon zest

1 tsp pure lemon extract

100g neutral/vegetable oil

215g heavy/double cream

60g ground almonds

10g poppy seeds

305g all-purpose/plain flour

7g baking powder

Pinch of salt

FOR THE SUGAR SYRUP

100g granulated/caster sugar

50g fresh lemon juice

50g water

FOR THE ICING

250g powdered/icing
  sugar, sifted

5g poppy seeds

Fresh lemon juice (from
  1–2 lemons)

SPECIAL EQUIPMENT

9 × 13-inch (23 × 33cm) cake
  pan/tin

Stand mixer, with the
  whisk attachment

Offset spatula

I think I could write a whole book just on lemon cakes! As good as this cake is, the tangy, crunchy icing you get on top finishes it off perfectly. This bake sits well for a few days, so you can leave it in the fridge before bringing it to room temperature and adding the icing.

1. Preheat the oven to 320°F/160°C. Lightly grease a 9 × 13-inch (23 × 33cm) pan with butter and line the base and sides with parchment paper, creating a slight overhang so you can lift the cake out once baked.

2. To make the cake, in the bowl of a stand mixer fitted with the whisk attachment, combine the eggs, sugar, lemon zest, and lemon extract. Whisk on medium speed for 2–3 minutes, or until the mixture is pale and thicker in consistency, scraping down the sides as needed.

3. Lower the speed to low and add the oil, then add the cream.

4. Add the ground almonds and poppy seeds. Mix until combined.

5. In a medium bowl, whisk together the flour, baking powder, and salt. Sift this mixture into the bowl of the stand mixer. Use a spatula to gently fold this into the batter. Keep mixing until the flour has absorbed, but be careful not to overbeat it. There might be a few small lumps, but don't worry about that. Pour the batter into the prepared pan.

6. Place the pan in the oven and bake for 40–45 minutes, or until it has a golden color and a skewer inserted in the center comes out clean.

7. To make the sugar syrup, in a small saucepan on the stovetop over low heat, combine the sugar, lemon juice, and water. Bring to a boil, then remove the saucepan from the heat and let it cool as the cake bakes.

8. Remove the pan from the oven and immediately pour the sugar syrup all over the cake. Allow the cake to cool in the pan for 5–10 minutes. Carefully lift the cake out, remove the parchment paper, and wrap the cake tightly in plastic wrap/cling film. Refrigerate overnight.

9. Remove the cake from the fridge and allow it to reach room temperature.

10. To make the icing, in a medium bowl, combine the sugar and poppy seeds. Add the juice from ½ a lemon and whisk this into the icing. Keep whisking in lemon juice until the mixture resembles the consistency of runny honey.

11. Use an offset spatula to spread the icing on the cake. Allow the cake to rest at room temperature for 1 hour to allow the icing to form a slight "crust" before serving.

TWO
TIER

Lemon and Yuzu Travel Cake

MAKES 1 LOAF CAKE

FOR THE CAKE

Unsalted butter, softened,
for greasing and piping

245g cake/pastry flour, plus
more for dusting

220g powdered/icing sugar

4g lemon zest

220g eggs

80g neutral/vegetable oil

¾ tsp lemon extract

170g heavy/double cream

50g ground almonds

5.5g baking powder

FOR THE SUGAR SYRUP

300g granulated/caster sugar

150g fresh lemon juice

150g water

½ batch Vanilla Mascarpone
Cream (page 218)

FOR THE GEL

125g fresh orange
juice, divided

10g yuzu juice

5g granulated/caster sugar

1g agar-agar powder

FOR THE ICING

100g powdered/icing sugar

Yuzu juice

As someone who loves anything citrus, yuzu is one of the flavors that I love to bake with. The versatility of the Tier 1 cake recipe (page 48) makes for a stellar loaf cake here, which is then elevated with decorative piping and yuzu gel. If you can't get hold of yuzu juice, just replace it with lemon juice.

1. Preheat the oven to 320°F/160°C. Lightly grease a 2-pound (900g) loaf pan with butter. Add a small amount of flour. Shake the flour around the pan to coat and then pour out the excess.

2. To make the cake, in the bowl of a stand mixer fitted with the whisk attachment, combine the sugar, lemon zest, and eggs. Whisk on medium for 2–3 minutes, scraping down the sides as needed. The mixture should be thicker and paler in consistency.

3. While whisking on low, slowly add the oil and lemon extract, then add the cream.

4. Add the ground almonds and continue to whisk until combined.

5. In a small bowl, combine the flour and baking powder. Sift this mixture into the bowl of the stand mixer. Whisk on low until there are no more dry bits. Don't worry if there are a few lumps, but be sure to not overmix. Pour the batter into the prepared pan.

6. Add a small amount of softened butter to a piping bag. Cut a small bit off the end and pipe a very thin line of butter lengthwise down the center of the batter. This will control the cracking as the cake bakes.

7. Place the pan in the oven and bake for about 70–80 minutes, or until a wooden skewer inserted in the center comes out clean.

8. Meanwhile, to make the sugar syrup, in a medium saucepan over medium heat, combine the sugar, lemon juice, and water. Bring the mixture to a boil, then immediately remove the saucepan from the heat and set aside.

9. Remove the pan from the oven. While the cake is still hot, carefully transfer it to a wire rack with a tray underneath. Use a wooden skewer to poke holes all over the cake, then soak the entire cake with the sugar syrup. A lot of syrup will run off the cake, but you really want to try to soak the cake because this will add moisture.

10. Immediately wrap the cake in plastic wrap/cling film and refrigerate overnight. This will allow the cake to absorb that moisture and soften the crumb.

2lb (900g) loaf pan/tin

Stand mixer, with the
  whisk attachment

3× piping bags, plus a 0.8-inch
  (20mm) round tip nozzle

Wooden skewer

Hand blender

Baking tray/sheet

11. Prepare the Vanilla Mascarpone Cream and refrigerate overnight.

12. To make the yuzu gel, squeeze fresh oranges and pass the juice through a sieve. Weigh 75g of orange juice.

13. In a small saucepan over medium heat, combine the orange juice, yuzu juice, sugar, and agar-agar powder. Bring it to a boil, then remove the saucepan from the heat and stir in the remaining 50g of orange juice.

14. Pour the mixture into a shallow tray and refrigerate for 30 minutes, or until firm to the touch. Remove the tray from the fridge and transfer the mixture to a small measuring jug. Use a hand blender to blend it to a smooth gel. Pour the gel into a piping bag and refrigerate until needed.

15. Preheat the oven to 355°F/180°C and remove the cake from the fridge.

16. To make the yuzu icing, to a small bowl, add the sugar. Whisk in yuzu juice until the mixture resembles the consistency of runny honey. Start with about 2 tablespoons of juice and add more as needed.

17. Use a pastry brush to brush a thick layer of icing around the entire cake. (You might not need it all.) Place the cake on a baking tray and bake for 3 minutes to set the glaze.

18. Remove the tray from the oven and allow the cake to cool to room temperature.

19. Add the Vanilla Mascarpone Cream to a stand mixer fitted with the whisk attachment and whisk until it reaches a medium-stiff peak. Add the mixture to a piping bag fitted with a 0.8-inch (20mm) round tip.

20. Pipe dollops of cream across the top of the cake. Gently heat the back of a small measuring spoon and carve out indents in a few of the dollops. Pipe the yuzu gel into the indents you just created.

21. Serve the cake at room temperature.

Blueberry and Almond Financiers

MAKES 8 FINANCIERS

140g unsalted butter, plus
more for greasing

185g egg whites

90g ground almonds

185g powdered/icing sugar

2g lemon zest

½ fresh vanilla bean or
1 tsp vanilla bean paste

90g self-rising/self-raising
flour, plus more for dusting

125g blueberries

Lightly toasted flaked
almonds, for topping

SPECIAL EQUIPMENT

Oval silicone mold/metal
pan/tin

Whenever I need a quick bake, these financiers are my go-to. The ground almonds bring a softness to the cake, but they can be replaced with any ground nut. You can also try swapping in different berries depending on what you have. I barely let these cool before I've eaten them all!

1. Preheat the oven to 320°F/160°C. If you're using a metal pan (or a cupcake pan), lightly grease it with butter. Add a small amount of flour. Shake the flour around the pan to coat and then pour out the excess.

2. In a small saucepan on the stovetop over low heat, melt the butter. Remove the saucepan from the heat and allow the butter to cool for 5 minutes.

3. In a medium bowl, whisk the egg whites for 30 seconds, or until frothy.

4. Add the ground almonds, sugar, and lemon zest. Cut the vanilla bean lengthways, and using the knife to scrape out half of the seeds, add these into the bowl. Whisk until combined.

5. Place a sieve over the medium bowl and sift in the flour. Whisk until the flour has just been absorbed, about 30 seconds.

6. Add the melted butter and whisk until there are no more streaks of butter.

7. Gently fold the blueberries into the batter.

8. Pour the batter into the cups of an oval silicone mold or metal pan (or the cups of a cupcake pan/tin) and fill the cups about ¾ full. Sprinkle a few flaked almonds over the top of each cup.

9. Place the pan in the oven and bake for 25–30 minutes, or until the financiers have a nice golden color.

10. Remove the pan from the oven and allow the financiers to cool for 5 minutes before removing them from the pan. Serve while still warm or allow them to cool completely and then serve later.

Brown Butter and Hazelnut Financier

**MAKES 1 LARGE
FINANCIER CAKE**

**FOR THE CHOCOLATE
CHANTILLY**

90g dark chocolate, 70%
cocoa solids, finely chopped

200g heavy/double cream

10g honey

FOR THE FINANCIER

75g whole hazelnuts, skin on,
plus more, to decorate

145g unsalted butter, plus
more for greasing

155g egg whites

3g orange zest

½ fresh vanilla bean pod or
1 tsp vanilla bean paste

155g powdered/icing sugar

75g self-rising/self-raising
flour, plus more for dusting

SPECIAL EQUIPMENT

Hand blender

1lb (450g) loaf pan/tin

Baking tray/sheet

2× piping bags, plus 1 large
grass tip nozzle

This is one of those cakes that you can't stop going back to, slice after slice. The process for making this bake is the same as the Tier 1 financiers (page 53), but we're doing one large-format cake instead of the more traditional miniature version. For Tier 2 we're ramping up the flavors by making a few simple swaps—adding roasted, ground hazelnuts instead of almonds, and brown butter instead of melted butter. The cake is decorated with a smooth chocolate chantilly, and then finished with a touch of elegance using the hazelnuts and their skins.

1. To make the chocolate chantilly, add the chocolate to a tall measuring jug/cup.

2. In a small saucepan on the stovetop over medium heat, combine the cream and honey. Stir occasionally until hot but not boiling, then immediately remove the saucepan from the heat and pour the mixture over the chocolate.

3. Allow the cream to sit for 2 minutes before using a hand blender to blend until smooth. Cover and refrigerate for 3 hours.

4. Preheat the oven to 320°F/160°C. Grease a 1-pound (450g) loaf pan with butter. Sprinkle flour in the pan and shake the pan to coat with flour. Tap the pan to remove any excess flour.

5. To make the financier, spread the hazelnuts on a baking tray. Place the tray in the oven and roast the hazelnuts for 8–12 minutes, or until the skins start to burst.

6. Remove the tray from the oven and let them cool slightly, then rub the hazelnuts between a kitchen/tea towel to remove the skins (save these for decoration). Don't worry if there are still a few skins remaining as this will give the cake batter a nice color. Place the skinned hazelnuts back into the oven for 5 minutes, or until they are a golden color.

7. Remove the tray from the oven and allow the hazelnuts to cool for 10–15 minutes. Add them to a blender and blend them into a fine powder. Set aside.

8. In a small saucepan on the stovetop over medium heat, melt the butter. Once the butter has melted, it will begin to roar quite violently, then big bubbles will form in the pan. After this, the bubbles will become much smaller and the pan will go very quiet. At this point, you're looking for a caramelized, nutty aroma coming from the pan. This should take around 3–4 minutes.

9. Remove the saucepan from the heat and measure out 115g. Allow the butter to cool for 5 minutes.

10. In a medium bowl, whisk together the egg whites for 30 seconds, or until they become frothy.

11. Add the ground hazelnuts, orange zest, and vanilla. Sift the sugar into the bowl. Whisk briefly until everything has been combined.

12. Sift the self-rising flour into the bowl. Briefly mix again to ensure the dry ingredients have been incorporated.

13. Whisk in the cooled brown butter. It might not incorporate right away, so keep whisking until it does. Pour the cake batter into the greased pan.

14. Add some softened butter to a piping bag. Cut a very small hole at the end of the bag and pipe a thin line of butter down the center of the batter.

15. Place the pan in the oven and bake for 60 minutes. It should have a nice golden color on top and a skewer inserted into the center should come out clean.

16. Transfer the pan to a wire rack and allow the cake to cool for 1–2 hours.

17. Remove the dark chocolate chantilly from the fridge and very briefly stir by hand just until it is smooth. Be careful not to over-work it. Add the chantilly to a piping bag fitted with a large grass tip nozzle.

18. Pipe long lines of the chantilly across the top of the cake, overlapping them slightly.

19. Finish by decorating the cake with the reserved roasted hazelnut halves, and hazelnut skins.

New York-Style Vanilla Cheesecake

MAKES 1 CHEESECAKE

FOR THE BASE

140g graham crackers/
  digestive biscuits

2g lemon zest

70g unsalted butter, melted,
  plus more for greasing

FOR THE FILLING

170g granulated/caster sugar

40g all-purpose/plain flour

900g full-fat cream
  cheese, cold

100g sour cream, cold

1 fresh vanilla bean or
  2 tsp vanilla bean paste

100g eggs

310g heavy/double
  cream, cold

Vanilla Chantilly, to serve
  (page 224)

SPECIAL EQUIPMENT

10-inch (25cm) cake pan/tin
  with a removable base

Blender

Stand mixer, with the
  paddle attachment

Deep roasting tray

If there's one dessert that is my go-to, it's this NY-style cheesecake. It's always highly requested by my family and because you can make it in advance, it's simple to pull out and serve. It's worth splashing out on good-quality vanilla beans to make the flavor really pop. If you have time, pull together a little berry compote to go with it too.

1. Preheat the oven to 320°F/160°C. Lightly grease the bottom of a 10-inch (25cm) cake pan with a removable base. Place a circle of parchment paper on the bottom. Wrap the entire pan with aluminum foil (I use heavy-duty foil because it's much larger and means there are no overlapping gaps where water can seep in.)

2. To make the base, in a blender, blend the crackers at a medium speed until they reach a fine crumb, ensuring there are no large lumps. Transfer the crumbs to a medium bowl and stir in the lemon zest.

3. Add 80% of the melted butter to the crumb mixture, stirring with a spatula. Add butter until the mixture resembles slightly wet sand. Be careful not to make it soggy.

4. Add the biscuit mixture to the prepared pan. Use a flat-bottomed glass or measuring cup/jug to smooth the mixture until perfectly even.

5. Place the pan in the oven and bake for 10 minutes. Remove the pan from the oven and allow the base to cool.

6. To make the filling, in a small bowl, thoroughly whisk together the sugar and flour until no lumps remain.

7. In the bowl of a stand mixer, combine the cream cheese, sour cream, and sugar mixture. Use a knife to split the vanilla bean lengthways and scrape out the seeds. Add the seeds to the bowl and mix on low speed for 2 minutes, or until no lumps of flour remain, scraping down the sides if needed.

8. Slowly add the eggs and continue to mix. Scrape down the sides of the bowl and mix again until everything has been incorporated.

9. Add the cream and mix for 1 minute more. Remove the bowl from the mixer and scrape the bottom with a spatula to loosen any lumps. Return the bowl to the mixer and mix on low speed for 1 minute more, or until the mixture is very smooth and lump-free. Air bubbles can cause the cheesecake to crack, so be careful not to mix too vigorously. Firmly tap the bowl on your work surface to get rid of any remaining air bubbles.

10. Place the cake pan in a deep roasting tray and place the tray in the oven. Carefully pour the cheesecake mixture on top of the biscuit base. Fill the roasting tray with boiling water until the water comes up to about ⅓ of the side of the cake pan.

11. Bake the cheesecake for 80 minutes. The cheesecake is done when there's a wobble in the center, about 3 inches (8cm) in diameter, when you gently shake the tray. It might seem like the cheesecake is undercooked, but residual heat will finish the cooking and this is the key to a velvety-smooth texture.

12. Remove the tray from the oven and remove the cake pan from the water bath. With the foil still attached to the pan, allow the cheesecake to cool at room temperature for 2 hours. Remove the foil and refrigerate uncovered overnight or for a minimum of 6 hours.

13. Carefully remove the cheesecake from the pan and use a warm palette knife to smooth the edges. Gently heat a sharp knife and cut the cheesecake into equal portions. Serve with Vanilla Chantilly or a berry compote.

TIER **ONE**

TWO
TIER

Passion Fruit Cheesecakes

MAKES 4 CHEESECAKES

FOR THE BISCUIT BASE

95g unsalted butter, cold and cubed

90g all-purpose/plain flour

60g ground almonds

50g granulated/caster sugar

1.5g baking powder

2g lemon zest

Pinch of sea salt

FOR THE CHEESECAKE

105g granulated/caster sugar

25g all-purpose/plain flour

540g full-fat cream cheese, cold

60g sour cream, cold

½ fresh vanilla bean or 1 tsp vanilla bean paste

60g eggs

125g heavy/double cream, cold

FOR THE PASSION FRUIT GEL

200g passion fruit purée

2g agar-agar

2 fresh passion fruits

Vanilla Chantilly, to serve (page 224)

Almost too pretty to eat, this passionfruit cheesecake uses the same base filling as the Tier 1 cheesecake (page 58) but with a homemade cookie base and a wafer-thin passionfruit gel on top. Making your own cookie base might seem like a lot of work, but trust me, this crust is addictive. Once it comes out of the oven, snap off a little piece and you'll see just how delicious it is. You'll never go back to store-bought cookies again!

1. Start with the biscuit base by adding all of the ingredients into the bowl of a stand mixer. Mix on a medium-low speed with the paddle attachment until the butter has broken down and it resembles a crumble.

2. Remove the bowl from the mixer and use your hands to squeeze the mixture together until it forms a dough.

3. Place the dough in between two silicone mats (or two sheets of parchment paper) and roll it out until it is relatively thin, using a rolling pin—don't worry about the shape. Place it in the freezer while you preheat the oven to 345°F/175°C.

4. Remove the dough from the freezer and lift the silicone mats onto a baking tray. Peel off the top mat, and bake for 20–25 minutes, or until it has a golden brown color. Remove it from the oven and let it cool completely before blending it into a fine crumb.

5. Place four 3.5 (D) × 2.4-inch (H) (8.9 × 6.1cm) tart rings onto a baking tray lined with a silicone mat. Spoon 30g of the biscuit crumb into the base of each mold and use a small glass to flatten it. Ensure it is completely flush with the ring mold to prevent the cheesecake mix from leaking. Save the remaining crumb to decorate the plate.

6. Place the biscuit bases into the oven, and bake for 8 minutes. Remove them from the oven to cool and lower the temperature to 285°F/140°C.

7. Into the bowl of a stand mixer, whisk together the sugar and flour for the cheesecake. Add the cream cheese, sour cream and vanilla. Mix on a low speed with the paddle attachment for 1–2 minutes, scraping down the sides as needed.

8. Pour in the eggs and let those incorporate, followed by the cream. Scrape the bottom of the bowl to ensure all the ingredients are fully combined. Then, firmly tap the bowl on the work surface to get rid of any air bubbles.

9. Add the mixture into a piping bag, and pipe 200g of batter into each ring mold.

Stand mixer, with the paddle
  attachment and the
  whisk attachment

2× silicone baking mats

Rolling pin

Blender

2× baking trays/sheets

4× 3.5 (W) × 2.4-inch (H)
  (8.9 × 6.1cm) tart rings

Piping bag

Heat gun/hair dryer

10. Place the tray into the oven (no water bath needed), and bake for around 30 minutes, or until there is a small wobble in the center of the cheesecakes, about ¾ inches (2cm). Remove the cheesecakes from the oven, and allow them to cool to room temperature before placing them in the fridge, uncovered, for 6 hours or overnight.

11. Add the passion fruit purée into a small saucepan along with the agar-agar. Over medium heat, whisk it together until it reaches a rolling boil. Remove it from the heat, and pour the mixture onto a tray lined with a silicone mat. Swirl the mixture around the tray so that you get a thin layer of the gel. Place it in the fridge for 30 minutes.

12. Meanwhile, cut the fresh passion fruits in half and scoop the fruit out into a small saucepan. Heat it for 1–2 minutes until it has dissolved, then pass the mixture through a sieve to catch the black seeds. Keep these to one side.

13. Remove a cheesecake from the fridge and use a heat gun to gently heat the sides of the ring mold. Carefully remove the ring and use a hot palette knife to smooth any rough edges. Lift the cheesecake onto your serving plate.

14. Remove the passion fruit gel from the fridge and use the ring mold from the cheesecake to cut a disk. Carefully lift this on to the top of the cheesecake. Take the seeds from the passionfruit and dot these over the top. Repeat the plating for the remaining cheesecakes.

15. Finish by taking some remaining biscuit crumbs and spooning these onto the plate. Add a quenelle of whipped Vanilla Chantilly and serve.

Tiramisu Pots

MAKES 6 POTS

FOR THE FILLING

450g mascarpone, cold

70g granulated/caster sugar

10g coffee liqueur (Kahlúa recommended)

75g egg yolks, cold

100g heavy/double cream, cold

FOR THE ASSEMBLY

36 ladyfinger biscuits, 220g total

250g hot coffee

Cocoa powder

SPECIAL EQUIPMENT

Stand mixer, with the whisk attachment

6× 5oz dessert cups

I'm a purist when it comes to most of my baking, but I'm cheating a little here with the addition of cream in my tiramisu. It's not traditional, but I really enjoy the texture it brings to the dessert. Try adding some orange zest to the cream or grated chocolate on top instead of cocoa powder. These pots are so simple to prep ahead of time, so just leave them in the fridge until you're ready to serve.

1. To make the mascarpone filling, in the bowl of a stand mixer fitted with the whisk attachment, combine all the filling ingredients. Whisk for 3–4 minutes or until the mixture has thickened and holds a medium peak.

2. Add the coffee to a small bowl, then dunk 2 biscuits. Submerge the biscuits long enough so they've completely absorbed the coffee and aren't crunchy in the middle—but not so soggy that they fall apart.

3. Break the biscuits into pieces and fit them snuggly in the bottom of a 5oz dessert cup so there are as few gaps as possible.

4. Spoon a layer of the mascarpone filling on top, about ¼ inch (0.6cm) thick, and then dust a very thin layer of cocoa powder over the filling. You just need a thin dusting, so you don't need to cover the entire cream with a thick layer of cocoa powder.

5. Repeat steps 2 through 4 until you finish with a layer of cream. Repeat this process for the remaining 5 pots. To get a very clean finish for the pot, use a palette knife to smooth the cream so it's completely flush with the top of the pot.

6. Refrigerate the cups for a minimum of 3–4 hours or ideally overnight.

7. Dust an even layer of cocoa powder over the top of the pots before serving.

Mocha Charlotte Cake

MAKES 1 CAKE

FOR THE LADY FINGERS

55g all-purpose/plain flour

55g cornstarch/corn flour

120g egg yolks

110g granulated/caster sugar, divided, plus extra for dusting

½ tsp vanilla bean paste

145g egg whites

Freshly brewed coffee

FOR THE MASCARPONE CREAM

225g mascarpone, cold

35g granulated/caster sugar

5g coffee liqueur (Kahlúa recommended)

35g egg yolks, cold

50g heavy/double cream, cold

FOR THE CHOCOLATE MOUSSE

160g heavy/double cream

60g whole milk

250g dark chocolate, 70% cocoa solids, chopped

50g egg yolks

125g egg whites

20g granulated/caster sugar

Pinch of flaky sea salt

Vanilla Chantilly (page 224), for serving

Chocolate curls, for decorating

Now, I'll admit whenever I make a charlotte cake, I don't usually make my own lady fingers, but there's great satisfaction in making them from scratch here. We are taking the filling from the Tier 1 tiramisu (page 64) and layering it with a rich chocolate mousse that pairs beautifully with the coffee-soaked sponge.

1. Preheat the oven to 355°F/180°C.

2. Take two large sheets of parchment paper and on one sheet, trace two circles, each 7.1 inches (18cm) in diameter. On the second sheet, draw two sets of lines (four lines total) that are 3 inches (7.6cm) tall and extend across the width of the paper, like train tracks. These will act as a guide to pipe your lady fingers. Place these sheets underneath silicone mats and onto two separate baking trays.

3. Sift the flour and cornstarch into a small bowl then set this to one side.

4. Add the egg yolks, 55g of sugar, and the vanilla bean paste into the bowl of a stand mixer. Whisk on medium speed until the mixture is very light and fluffy and it holds a ribbon when you drizzle the batter—it will take 3–5 minutes. Transfer to a bowl and set aside.

5. Add the egg whites into the bowl of a stand mixer and whisk on medium-low speed. Once the mixture is thick and starts to hold a medium peak, slowly add in the remaining sugar and whisk until you have a stiff meringue, about 1–2 minutes.

6. Working quickly, fold the meringue into the egg yolk mixture, ⅓ at a time, and stop as soon as there is no more visible meringue. Finally, fold in the flour mixture and stir together just until there are no more dry bits. Be careful not to over mix this or you will knock out the air. Add the mixture into a piping bag fitted with a 0.5-inch (12mm) round tip nozzle.

7. In a tight spiral motion, pipe two disks of batter onto the prepared guides.

8. With the remaining batter, pipe 22–25 lady fingers (at minimum) on the second guide, leaving about 0.5-inch (12mm) between each one as they will spread slightly.

9. Dust the tops lightly with sugar and immediately place them in the oven, with the fingers on the middle-upper rack (to give them color) and the disks on the middle-lower rack. Bake the fingers for 17–18 minutes, or until golden and slightly cracked on top. Leave the discs a few minutes longer to color. Once cooled, wrap the fingers in a container and freeze them.

3× baking trays/sheets

3× silicone mats

Stand mixer, with the whisk
attachment

Piping bag with a 0.5-inch
(12mm) round
tip nozzle

Hand blender

7 × 2.4-inch (18 × 6cm)
metal ring mold

Acetate

Hair dryer/heat gun

10. For the mascarpone cream, add all of the ingredients into the bowl of a stand mixer with the whisk attachment, and mix on medium-low speed until it is smooth and has a medium peak. Transfer to a bowl and set aside.

11. For the chocolate mousse, heat the cream and milk in a small saucepan over medium heat. Meanwhile, add the chopped chocolate into a tall measuring jug/cup.

12. Once the cream is steaming, pour this over the chocolate and let it sit for 2 minutes before blending with a hand blender until smooth. Pour this into a medium bowl and whisk in the egg yolks.

13. Add the egg whites into the bowl of a stand mixer and whisk on medium-low speed until thick and frothy. Slowly add the sugar, and salt, and continue whisking until you have a medium-stiff peak.

14. Add ⅓ of the meringue to the chocolate base and whisk it until there are no more lumps of meringue. Fold the remaining meringue in, in two additions until you have a smooth mixture.

15. Place a 7 × 2.4-inch (18 × 6cm) metal ring mold onto a baking tray lined with a silicone mat. Line the inside with acetate, ensuring it is completely flush with the height of the ring.

16. If needed, trim the lady finger disks around the edges so that they fit inside the ring. Place one disk on the base and pour over ½ the brewed coffee, to lightly soak it. Top the soaked disk with the mascarpone; spread this out evenly. Add in the second disk and pour over the remaining coffee, to lightly soak it. Top with the chocolate mousse. Use a palette knife to smooth the mousse so it is flush with the ring mold, and freeze it overnight.

17. Transfer the frozen cake onto your serving plate and gently heat the ring mold, using a hairdryer or heat gun, to lift it off. Peel off the acetate.

18. Let the cake come to room temperature for about 3 hours before removing your lady fingers from the freezer. Carefully trim the bottom of the fingers so they are all the same height and have a flat bottom. Place them around the outside of the cake.

19. Finish the cake with Vanilla Chantilly on top and some chocolate curls, for decoration. Let the assembled cake sit at room temperature for a few minutes so the lady fingers can warm up before you serve it.

Chocolate Chunk Brownies

MAKES 1 PAN OF BROWNIES

220g unsalted butter

320g dark chocolate, 70% cocoa solids

200g eggs

20g egg yolks

85g granulated/caster sugar

185g light brown sugar

150g all-purpose/plain flour

30g cocoa powder

½ tsp sea salt flakes, plus more for topping

40g chocolate chunks, 70% cocoa solids

100g milk chocolate, for drizzling

SPECIAL EQUIPMENT

9 × 9-inch (23 × 23cm) baking pan/tin

Stand mixer, with the whisk attachment

Piping bag

My mum's brownie recipe is a family classic, but I've adapted it here with the addition of a stunning crinkly finish. Whisking the eggs and sugar whips air into the batter, which, once baked, gives the brownie a thin, almost meringue like, texture on top.

1. Preheat the oven to 355°F/180°C. Grease a 9 × 9-inch (23 × 23cm) baking pan and line the inside with parchment paper, creating a slight overhang so you can lift the brownies out once baked.

2. In a medium bowl, combine the butter and chocolate. Place the bowl over a pot of gently simmering water. Stir the mixture occasionally until it has melted. Remove the bowl from the pot and cool for 10 minutes. It's a really important step to prevent the eggs from scrambling when you add them.

3. In the large bowl of a stand mixer with the whisk attachment, combine the eggs, egg yolks, granulated sugar, and brown sugar. Whisk for 3–4 minutes or until the mixture becomes pale and fluffy. (You can also mix these ingredients with an electric hand mixer.)

4. Once it is thick, very slowly drizzle in the cooled melted chocolate mixture while still whisking on a low speed. It's important to do this slowly so the eggs can slowly adjust to the temperature of the warm chocolate.

5. Once the chocolate has completely incorporated, sieve in the flour, cocoa powder, and salt. Use a hand whisk to gently mix these in until no more dry ingredients are visible. Don't overmix.

6. Pour the batter into the pan, spreading it to the edges. Sprinkle the chocolate chunks and a pinch of sea salt flakes over the top.

7. Place the pan in the oven and bake for 24–27 minutes. A wooden skewer inserted in the middle should still come out slightly wet.

8. Remove the pan from the oven and allow the brownies to cool to room temperature. Refrigerate for 30 minutes.

9. Meanwhile, in a medium bowl, add the milk chocolate. Place the bowl over a pot of gently simmering water. Stir the mixture occasionally until it has completely melted. Add the chocolate to a piping bag.

10. Carefully lift the cooled brownies from the pan. Cut a small hole in the tip of the piping bag and quickly drizzle the chocolate across the brownies in a zigzag motion.

11. Use a hot knife to cut the into squares before serving.

Triple Chocolate Brownie Fingers

MAKES 8-10 BROWNIE FINGERS

1 batch Whipped Chocolate Ganache (page 223)

FOR THE BROWNIE

220g unsalted butter

320g dark chocolate, 70% cocoa solids

200g eggs

20g egg yolks

85g granulated/caster sugar

185g light brown sugar

150g all-purpose/plain flour

30g cocoa powder

½ tsp flaky sea salt, plus extra for topping

FOR THE CHOCOLATE COATING

300g dark chocolate, 70% cocoa solids

30g neutral/vegetable oil

This is one of those desserts that looks so elegant from the piping, but is sneaky-easy to pull together. Using the same brownie recipe from Tier 1 (page 69), we dress it up using a simple chocolate glaze around the outside and then pipe a Whipped Chocolate Ganache (page 223) on top. For a different flavor combination, try swapping in the Whipped Vanilla Ganache (page 222).

1. Prepare the Whipped Chocolate Ganache and chill this in the fridge for a minimum of 6 hours, or ideally overnight.

2. Preheat the oven to 355°F/180°C. Grease a 9 × 9 inch (23 × 23cm) baking pan and line the inside with parchment paper, creating a slight overhang so you can lift the brownies out once baked.

3. In a medium bowl, combine the butter and chocolate. Place the bowl over a pot of gently simmering water. Stir the mixture occasionally until it has completely melted. Remove the bowl from the pot and allow the mixture to cool for 10 minutes. It's a really important step to prevent the eggs from scrambling when you add them.

4. In the large bowl of a stand mixer with the whisk attachment, combine the eggs, egg yolks, granulated sugar, and light brown sugar. Whisk for 3–4 minutes or until the mixture becomes pale and fluffy. This is the secret to getting that nice shiny top on your brownies. (You can also mix these ingredients with an electric hand mixer.)

5. Once it is thick, very slowly drizzle in the cooled melted chocolate mixture while still whisking on a low speed. It's important to do this slowly so the eggs can slowly adjust to the temperature of the warm chocolate.

6. Once the chocolate has completely incorporated, sift in the flour, cocoa powder, and salt. Use a hand whisk to gently mix these in until no more dry ingredients are visible. Don't overmix.

7. Pour the batter into the pan, spreading it to the edges. Sprinkle a pinch of sea salt flakes over the top.

8. Place the pan in the oven and bake for 24–27 minutes. A wooden skewer inserted in the middle should still come out slightly wet.

9. Remove the pan from the oven and allow to cool to room temperature, then place in the fridge for 1 hour.

9 × 9 inch (23 × 23cm) baking pan/tin

Stand mixer, with the whisk attachment

Instant read thermometer

2× silicone mats

Piping bag with a #4B star tip nozzle

10. Carefully lift the cooled brownies out of the tray and use a hot knife to cut them into rectangular slices. Depending on how big you would like them, you should be able to get 8–10 slices. Place these in the fridge.

11. For the chocolate coating, add the chocolate and oil to a medium bowl, and place it over a saucepan of gently simmering water. Stir until completely melted then remove it from the heat. Allow the mixture to cool to 104–113°F (40–45°C) then pour it into a small rectangular container, deep enough for you to be able to dip the brownies in.

12. Remove a brownie from the fridge, and placing a knife into the center, dip the brownie into the chocolate glaze, so that it just reaches the top edge of the brownie and then transfer it over to a silicone mat. Rub the brownie along the silicon mat to get rid of any excess chocolate on the bottom then transfer it to a clean silicone mat to set. Repeat with the remaining brownies.

13. Add the Whipped Chocolate Ganache to a bowl and whisk until you have a medium peak, being careful not to over whip it. Add the mixture into a piping bag fitted with a #4B star tip nozzle.

14. In an anti-clockwise motion, pipe a tight spiral of the ganache across the top of the brownie. Repeat this with the remaining brownies.

15. Allow them to sit at room temperature for 30 minutes before serving.

Chocolate Soufflé

MAKES 4 SOUFFLÉS

FOR THE BEURRE MANIÉ

50g unsalted butter, softened, plus more for greasing

55g all-purpose/plain flour

1g sea salt

FOR THE SOUFFLÉ BASE

270g whole milk

50g granulated/caster sugar, plus more for dusting

195g chopped dark chocolate, 70% cocoa solids

115g egg yolks

FOR THE MERINGUE

180g egg whites

3g freshly squeezed lemon juice

70g granulated/caster sugar

SPECIAL EQUIPMENT

4× 3.5 × 2-inch (9 × 5.5cm) ramekins

Electric hand mixer

Piping bag with a large round tip nozzle

Do I dare say this soufflé has never failed me? It might be risky to jinx a soufflé, but this dessert delivers on beauty and taste every time. The soufflé has the perfect rise, and is light with a rich chocolate flavor. Every baker has to have a chocolate soufflé in their locker and this is the one to show off your baking skills.

1. Preheat the oven to 320°F/160°C using the convection/fan-assisted setting.

2. Use a pastry brush to brush the insides of four 3.5 × 2-inch (9 × 5.5cm) ramekins with the softened unsalted butter, ensuring to stroke upward with the brush.

3. Sprinkle a small amount of sugar in the ramekins and swirl the sugar around to coat the ramekins. Tap the ramekins to remove any excess sugar. Set aside.

4. To make the beurre manié, in a medium bowl, combine the butter, flour, and salt. Use a spatula to beat until a thick, dry paste forms. Set aside.

5. To make the soufflé base, in a medium saucepan on the stovetop over medium heat, combine the milk and sugar. Bring the mixture to a gentle simmer.

6. Remove the saucepan from the heat and whisk in the beurre manié. Keep whisking until the beurre manié has broken down and been absorbed into the milk. About 30 seconds.

7. Return the saucepan to the heat and whisk for 1–2 minutes until the mixture has thickened. When you lift the mixture with the whisk, it should be slightly elastic in consistency and not too runny.

8. Remove the saucepan from the heat and whisk in the chopped dark chocolate until completely melted.

9. Transfer the mixture to a large bowl and add the egg yolks. Beat with a spatula until the eggs have been completely combined. Set aside.

10. To make the meringue, in a medium bowl, combine the egg whites and lemon juice. Whisk with an electric hand mixer on a medium-low speed until frothy, then slowly add the sugar 1 tablespoon at a time.

11. Increase the speed of the hand whisk to medium-high and whisk until the meringue has stiff peaks.

12. Fold the meringue into the soufflé base in three stages, ensuring you scoop the bottom of the bowl and there are no streaks of meringue left.

13. Transfer the mixture to a piping bag fitted with a large round tip nozzle.

14. Use the piping bag to fill the ramekins with the mixture. Use an offset spatula to completely smooth the tops so the mixture is flush with the rims of the ramekins. Use your thumb to carefully create a very small lip around the inside edge of each ramekin. Clean the outsides of the ramekins of any of the mixture.

15. Place the ramekins in the oven and bake for about 18–20 minutes. They should be well risen above the rim.

16. Remove the ramekins from the oven and serve immediately.

Peach Crumble Soufflé

MAKES 4 SOUFFLÉS

FOR THE CRUMBLE

30g flour

30g unsalted butter, cold
and cubed

30g ground almonds

30g granulated/caster sugar

Pinch of sea salt

2g lemon zest

**FOR THE ROASTED
PEACHES**

3 peaches

Honey

Light brown sugar

FOR THE SOUFFLÉ BASE

Unsalted butter, softened,
for greasing

Granulated/caster sugar,
for dusting

135g peach purée

25g passion fruit purée

15g granulated/caster sugar

7g cornstarch/corn flour

7g potato starch

FOR THE MERINGUE

110g egg whites

80g granulated/caster sugar

Créme Anglaise, to serve
(Page 208)

Growing up, my dad would serve homemade peach crumble almost every Sunday. The flavors are very nostalgic for me, so I wanted to take inspiration from that for this soufflé. We use the same techniques as in Tier 1—creating a flavored base and then folding meringue through— then advance it by adding a roasted peach layer, crumble topping, and crème anglaise.

1. For the crumble, add all of the ingredients into a medium bowl, and use your hands to rub the mixture between your fingers. Once the mixture has broken down and you have a crumble texture, pour it onto a baking tray and place it in the freezer for 10 minutes.

2. Preheat the oven to 345°F/175°C, then place the tray into the oven and bake for 10–15 minutes, occasionally stirring, until it is a light golden color. Set it aside to cool completely, then place it into a food processor and quickly pulse it to a fine crumb. Leave it at room temperature until you are ready to use it.

3. Increase the oven to 390°F/200°C and slice the peaches in half. Remove the stone from the center and place them skin-side down on a baking tray.

4. Drizzle some honey over the top of the peaches and add a sprinkling of light brown sugar. Bake for 30 minutes, or until caramelized around the edges. Remove the tray from the oven and allow the peaches to cool for 30 minutes.

5. Meanwhile, for the soufflé base add the sugar and starches to a small bowl and whisk them to combine.

6. Add the fruit purées into a medium saucepan and place it over medium heat. Once it reaches 104°F/40°C on an instant read thermometer, add in the sugar mixture and whisk until it comes to a boil. Once boiling, cook for a further 2 minutes, before transferring it into a small bowl. Cover the surface directly with plastic wrap/cling film and refrigerate it for 30 minutes, or until cool to the touch.

7. Use a pastry brush to brush the insides of four 3.5 × 2-inch (9 × 5.5cm) ramekins with softened unsalted butter, using upward brushstrokes. Add in some sugar, swirl it around to coat the inside, and then tip out any excess and then set them aside.

8. Take the cooled peaches, and use a knife to chop them into small cubes. They will be slightly soft so don't worry too much about the shape. Scoop the peaches into the base of each ramekin, splitting the amount evenly.

2× baking trays/sheets

Food processor

Instant read thermometer

4× 3.5 × 2-inch
  (9 × 5.5cm) ramekins

Stand mixer, with the
  whisk attachment

Piping bag

9. Remove the soufflé base from the fridge and add it into a large bowl; it should now be cool. Whisk it briefly to loosen the mixture. Preheat your oven to 320°F/160°C, using the convection/fan-assisted function (don't worry, the fan won't blow over your soufflés).

10. Into the bowl of a stand mixer, add the egg whites and sugar, and place this over a pan of gently simmering water, on a medium heat.

11. Whisk the mixture constantly until it reaches 113°F/45°C on a digital thermometer. Remove it from the heat and place it onto your stand mixer. Whisk on a medium speed for 5 minutes, or until the bowl is cool and the meringue holds a very stiff peak.

12. Add ⅓ of the meringue to the souffle basé, and whisk it gently until there are no more lumps.

13. Add the remaining meringue in two parts, using a spatula to gently fold it in until there are no more streaks of meringue.

14. Add the mixture into a piping bag, and snip a large hole off the end. Pipe the mixture to the top of each ramekin, then use a palette knife to completely smooth it, so that the mixture is flush with the ramekin.

15. Sprinkle an even layer of the crumble on top, and immediately place the soufflés into the oven. Bake for 14–17 minutes, or until the soufflés have risen and the crumble is golden around the edges.

16. Remove them from the oven and serve immediately with Créme Anglaise.

CHAPTER 4

pastry

My Dad's Lemon Tart

MAKES 1 TART

FOR THE FILLING

350g eggs

220g granulated/caster sugar

260g heavy/double cream

4g lemon zest

105g fresh lemon juice

FOR THE PASTRY

1 batch Lemon Pastry
  (page 28)

Crème fraîche, for serving

SPECIAL EQUIPMENT

Hand blender

9-inch (23cm) fluted tart pan/
  tin with a removable base

Instant read thermometer

Baking tray/sheet

Blowtorch

I have to say, this is the greatest lemon tart you'll ever eat. Believe me, I've tried to find better, but nothing compares. This is a recipe I grew up with, which I made a few small improvements to (sorry Dad!), giving it the perfect balance of citrus and sweet, with an incredibly smooth finish. I often serve it with crème fraîche, or for some crunch, brulée the top with sugar.

1. To make the lemon filling, combine the eggs, sugar, and cream in a tall measuring jug/cup. Blend until smooth using a hand blender.

2. Add the lemon zest and juice, and blend immediately (avoid adding too much air into the mixture and don't let the lemon juice sit in the mixture without blending, or it could curdle). Once smooth, cover with plastic wrap/. cling film and refrigerate..

3. Prepare the lemon pastry in a 9-inch (23cm) fluted tart pan with a removable base. Blind-bake and egg wash it until golden then set it aside while you finish the filling. Lower the oven temperature to 230°F/110°C.

4. Remove the lemon filling from the fridge and use a spoon to skim off all the foamy bubbles on the top.

5. To a saucepan on the stovetop over a medium-low heat, add the filling and heat until it reaches about 104°F/40°C. By heating it just slightly, we can lower the overall cooking time in the oven.

6. Immediately remove the pan from the heat and scoop off any air bubbles/ foam that might appear. Pour the filling through a sieve and back into a tall measuring jug.

7. Place the tart shell onto a baking tray. Place the tray in the center of the oven and very carefully pour the filling into the tart shell just until it reaches the top of the pastry. Use a blowtorch to very gently torch the top of the filling where any bubbles appear.

8. Bake the tart for 50–55 minutes, or until there is a very small wobble in the center of the tart. Immediately remove the tray from the oven and allow the tart to cool at room temperature for an hour. Then place the tart in the fridge, uncovered, for 3–4 hours.

9. Remove it from the tart pan and use a very hot knife to cut the tart into individual slices before serving. It is best served on the same day with crème fraîche.

Lemon Marmalade Tarts

MAKES 4 TARTS

FOR THE LEMON MARMALADE

100g lemons

Pinch of sea salt

15g fresh lemon juice

38g granulated/caster sugar

FOR THE PASTRY

1 batch Lemon Pastry
  (page 28)

FOR THE ALMOND CREAM

100g unsalted butter, soft

100g powdered/icing sugar

75g eggs

12g cornstarch/corn flour

100g ground almonds

2g lemon zest

FOR THE LEMON FILLING

100g heavy/double cream

80g granulated/caster sugar

130g eggs

35g fresh lemon juice

2g lemon zest

1 batch Whipped Vanilla
  Ganache (page 222)

Edible flowers, to decorate

Here we are elevating the Tier 1 lemon tart (page 82), and layering it with modern French pastry flavors and textures by adding a citrus-almond cream and lemon marmalade. The difficulty lies in the decorative finish, which adds height and texture from the piping, along with pops of color from the edible flowers. You can easily scale this up and make it as one large tart.

1. For the marmalade, roughly cut the lemons with the skin on (but remove the tips) into small pieces (about ¾-inch [2cm]) and place them into a small saucepan. Add just enough cold water to the pan to cover the lemons. Place it over medium heat until it reaches a rolling boil.

2. Once boiling, strain the lemons immediately, rinse them with cold water, and then place them back into the pan. Cover them with cold water again and bring to a boil once more.

3. Once boiled, strain and rinse again and add them back into the pan one final time with cold water, the lemon juice, and the salt. Bring to a simmer and cook for about 10 minutes, by which point the skins should be softer.

4. Strain the lemons and rinse with cold water.

5. Add them to a tall measuring jug/cup, add the sugar, and blend with a hand blender until it forms a thick, sticky mixture and there are no big lumps of lemon. Cover it and place it in the fridge to use later.

6. Prepare the lemon pastry for four 5 × 0.8-inch (12.7 × 2cm) perforated tart rings. These tart rings are larger than what is demonstrated in the techniques section, so note that you will need to re-roll any scraps of dough to ensure you have enough to make 4 tarts as well as the decorations. To line the walls of the tart rings, you will need strips of dough that are 15.7 × 0.9 inches (39.8 × 2.2cm).

7. You are not going to blind-bake the dough, so once you have lined the rings with the pastry, refrigerate them on a tray until you've made the almond cream. Preheat the oven to 345°F/175°C.

8. With the remaining dough, cut 4 rectangles out, roughly 2 × 0.5 inches (5 × 1cm), as well as some small circles, using the large end of a round tip piping nozzle. We will use these as decorations. Place them onto a perforated baking tray, lined with a perforated baking mat. Place a second perforated mat on top and bake for 8–10 minutes, or until golden. The small disks will bake faster, so you may need to take these out early. Set these both aside to cool.

Hand blender

4× 5 (W) × 0.8-inch (H)
(12.7 × 2cm) perforated
tart rings

Perforated baking tray/sheet

2× perforated baking mats

Stand mixer, with the paddle
attachment

2× piping bags, plus a round
tip piping nozzle and a #127
piping nozzle

9. For the almond cream, add the butter and sugar into a stand mixer fitted with a paddle attachment. Beat on medium speed for 2 minutes, pausing to scrape down the sides, as needed, until the mixture is smooth.

10. With the mixer still running, slowly pour in the eggs, adding them in stages. Once you've added all the eggs, scrape the bowl down and mix again for another minute. Don't worry if they look like they haven't fully incorporated.

11. Finally, add in the cornstarch, ground almonds, and lemon zest. Beat until everything is fully incorporated. Add the mixture into a piping bag.

12. Remove the chilled tart shells from the fridge. Holding a knife perpendicular to the edge of the pastry, trim off any excess dough. Use scissors to snip off roughly ½ inch (1.3cm) from the end of the piping bag. Pipe the cream into the base of the tart shells, filling them up about ⅓ of the way (about 75g of cream per tart, if you can weigh it).

13. Place them in the oven for 17–20 minutes, or until the almond cream is lightly golden on top.

14. Remove the tray from the oven and allow the tarts to cool for 5 minutes before carefully removing the tart rings.

15. Prepare the egg wash and use a pastry brush to brush a thin layer on the edges of the tart shells. Place them back in the oven and bake for a further 10–12 minutes or, until the tart is golden. Remove them from the oven to cool just slightly, and lower the oven to 230°F/110°C.

16. For the lemon filling, add the eggs, cream, and sugar into a tall measuring jug and blend until smooth with a hand blender.

17. Zest and juice the lemons then pour them into the mixture and blend it immediately, avoiding adding too much air into the mixture. Scoop off any excess foam with a spoon and set it to one side.

18. Take the lemon marmalade and spoon a small amount on top of a cooled tart, spreading a thin layer out using the back of a spoon. Repeat this for the remaining tarts.

19. Next, place the tarts into the oven and carefully pour in the lemon filling to the top of the tart shell. Bake them for about 15–20 minutes, or until they have a small wobble in the center. Remove them from the oven and cool to room temperature, before placing them into the fridge for 2 hours.

20. To finish the tarts, whip the Vanilla Whipped Ganache to a medium peak and add it into a piping bag fitted with a #127 nozzle.

21. Take a rectangle of pastry, and use a microplane to shave it down so that it fits neatly on the edge of the tart, but don't place it there yet.

22. Holding the piping bag at a 45° angle and with the thin end of the #127 nozzle facing up, pipe a zigzag of cream. Repeat this with the remaining rectangles and decorate the cream with edible flowers and the small circles of pastry.

23. Use a palette knife to carefully lift the pastry onto the top of the lemon tart and then serve.

Decadent Baked Chocolate Tart

MAKES 1 TART

FOR THE PASTRY

1 batch Chocolate Pastry
   (page 28)

FOR THE FILLING

155g eggs

85g granulated/caster sugar

Pinch of sea salt

180g heavy/double cream

325g whole milk

130g dark chocolate, 70%
   cocoa solids, melted

Cocoa powder, for decorating

Vanilla Chantilly (page 224),
   for serving

SPECIAL EQUIPMENT

9-inch (23cm) fluted
   tart pan/tin with a
   removable base

Baking tray/sheet

I've always found traditional chocolate ganache tarts to be too heavy, so here the filling is almost custard-like, giving it a soft, melt-in-the-mouth texture. The tart shines on its own, but isn't overly sweet, so I'd recommend pairing it with a spoonful of Vanilla Chantilly (page 224).

1. Prepare the Chocolate Pastry, blind-baking it in a 9-inch (22.8cm) fluted tart pan with a removable base. Once egg washed and baked, lower the oven temperature to 285°F/140°C.

2. To make the filling, in a medium bowl, whisk together the eggs, sugar, and salt for 1 minute.

3. In a small saucepan on the stovetop over medium heat, combine the cream and milk. Bring the mixture to a gentle simmer, then slowly pour it over the egg mixture and whisk constantly until combined.

4. Place the melted chocolate in a medium bowl and slowly pour the hot cream mixture over the chocolate, using a spatula to stir in small circles in the center of the bowl (ensure the melted chocolate is warm for this step). Use a spoon to scoop off any foam from the top.

5. Place the baked tart case, still in the pan, on a baking tray in the center of the oven. Carefully pour the chocolate filling into the tart shell, filling it just below the lip of the tart shell. Bake for about 50–60 minutes, or until there's a wobble about 3 inches (7.5cm) big in the center of the tart.

6. Remove the tray from the oven and allow the tart to cool to room temperature before placing it in the fridge for 2 hours.

7. Remove the tart from the fridge and pop it out of the pan and onto your serving plate. Decorate the tart with a dusting of cocoa powder around the edges. Serve with Vanilla Chantilly.

TIER **ONE**

Chocolate and Caramel Tartlets

MAKES 6 TARTLETS

FOR THE NAMELAKA

3g powdered gelatin

18g cold water

160g dark chocolate, 70% cocoa solids

120g whole milk

12g glucose syrup

240g heavy/double cream, cold

FOR THE PASTRY

1 batch Chocolate Pastry (page 28)

FOR THE FILLING

80g dark chocolate, 70% cocoa solids

100g eggs

50g granulated/caster sugar

Pinch of sea salt

200g whole milk

110g heavy/double cream

½ batch Salted Caramel (page 215), room temperature

This tart feels like something out of a fancy bakery. We keep the chocolate filling the same as Tier 1, but take it to the next level with a delicate chocolate namelaka piped around the outside, and a luscious salted caramel center. The balance of sweet and salty, along with the creamy textures, makes this the perfect bite.

1. To make the chocolate namelaka, in a small bowl, combine the powdered gelatin and cold water. Mix well and allow to bloom for 5 minutes.

2. To a medium bowl, add the chocolate and place the bowl over a pan of gently simmering water. Stir until the chocolate has completely melted. Remove the bowl from the heat and set aside.

3. In a small saucepan over medium heat, combine the milk and glucose. Stir the mixture until steaming. Remove the saucepan from the heat and stir in the bloomed gelatin until it completely dissolves.

4. Slowly pour this mixture over the melted chocolate, stirring in small circles in the center of the chocolate as you pour. Initially, the mixture will look quite split and oily, but as you add the remaining milk, everything will pull together.

5. Add the cold cream and use a hand blender or a hand whisk to mix until combined. Cover the surface with plastic wrap/cling film and refrigerate for a minimum of 5 hours or ideally overnight.

6. Prepare the Chocolate Pastry for six 3 × 0.8 inch (7.6 × 2cm) perforated tart rings. Blind-bake and egg wash the tartlets, then set them aside while you prepare the filling. Lower the oven to 285°F/140°C.

7. To make the chocolate filling, to a medium bowl, add the chocolate and place the bowl over a pan of gently simmering water. Stir until the chocolate has completely melted. Remove the bowl from the heat and set aside.

8. In a medium bowl, whisk together the eggs, sugar, and salt for 1 minute.

9. In a small saucepan over a medium heat, combine the milk and cream. Heat until the mixture is steaming.

10. Slowly pour the milk mixture over the eggs, whisking to combine as you pour.

11. Slowly pour this mixture over the melted chocolate, using a spatula to stir the mixture in small circles in the center as you pour. Once everything has been combined, use a spoon to scoop off any foamy bubbles on the top.

Hand blender

6× 3 (W) × 0.8-inch (H)
(7.6 × 2cm) perforated
tart rings

Stand mixer, with the
whisk attachment

2× piping bags, plus a #127
tip piping nozzle

12. Place the tray with the tarts on it, in the middle of the oven and carefully pour in the chocolate filling—just to the top of the tart shell. Bake for about 25–30 minutes, or until they have a very small wobble in the center.

13. Remove the tarts from the oven and allow them to cool to room temperature before refrigerating for 3 hours.

14. Remove the namelaka from the fridge and add it to the bowl of a stand mixer fitted with the whisk attachment. Whisk on medium speed until you get a medium-stiff peak.

15. Add the mixture to a piping bag fitted with a #127 nozzle. Holding the piping bag at a 45° angle, pipe the namelaka around the outside edge of the tart in a zigzag motion, leaving a small gap in the center. If you have a cake turntable, this can make it a little easier to spin the tart as you pipe.

16. Add the Salted Caramel to a piping bag and snip a small hole off the end. Pipe this into the center of the tart.

17. Allow the tarts to sit at room temperature for 30 minutes before serving.

Lemon-Glazed Madeleines

MAKES 12 MADELEINES

FOR THE MADELEINES

100g unsalted butter, plus
   more for greasing

100g powdered/icing sugar

5g baking powder

120g eggs

3g lemon zest

100g all-purpose/plain flour,
   plus more for dusting

FOR THE GLAZE

150g powdered/icing sugar

45g fresh lemon juice

SPECIAL EQUIPMENT

Instant read thermometer

Madeleine mold

2× piping bags, plus a 0.5 inch
   (13mm) round tip nozzle

Baking tray/sheet

A madeleine, for me, is the ultimate Sunday morning treat. The glaze adds a burst of lemon flavor and a tiny bit of crunch. I prep them the night before, ready to be served warm the next day.

1. Melt the butter in a small saucepan over low heat. Remove the saucepan from the heat and allow the butter to cool to 104°C/40°C.

2. In a small bowl, sift the sugar and baking powder.

3. In a medium bowl, combine the eggs and lemon zest. Add the sugar and baking powder mixture. Whisk until just combined.

4. Sift in the flour and whisk to mix until just combined. Add the cooled butter to the batter. Whisk until the butter has been fully incorporated.

5. Cover the surface with plastic wrap/cling film and refrigerate for a minimum of 6 hours. They say the longer you chill the dough, the bigger the hump!

6. Preheat the oven to 465°F/240°C.

7. Brush the insides of a madeleine mold with a thin layer of softened butter. Use a small sieve to sift flour over each cavity, then tap the tray firmly on the counter to eliminate any excess flour.

8. Remove the madeleine batter from the fridge and add it to a piping bag fitted with a 0.5-inch (13mm) round tip nozzle. Pipe the batter into the madeleine mold, filling each cavity about two-thirds of the way. Avoid overfilling the mold or the batter could spill out as it bakes.

9. Place the madeleine mold in the oven and immediately lower the temperature to 355°F/180°C. Bake the madeleines for 10–11 minutes, or until lightly golden around the edges and they have a nice hump in the center.

10. Remove the mold from the oven. While the madeleines are still warm, turn the tray on its side and tap it firmly to release the madeleines. Place the madeleines on a wire rack with a baking tray underneath.

11. Raise the temperature back to 465°F/240°C.

12. To make the glaze, sift the sugar into a small bowl, then pour the lemon juice over the top. Whisk until the mixture is smooth. Add the glaze to a piping bag and snip a small hole off the end.

13. With the hump facing up, pipe enough glaze over the top of each madeleine to coat it.

14. Place the baking tray in the oven for 1 minute. Remove the sheet from the oven and serve immediately. These are best eaten fresh and hot!

TIER **ONE**

Tiger Madeleines

MAKES 12 MADELEINES

FOR THE MADELEINES

1 fresh vanilla pod

170g powdered/icing sugar

8.5g baking powder

205g egg

170g all-purpose/plain flour,
  plus more for dusting

170g unsalted butter, plus
  more for greasing

7g cocoa powder

**FOR THE CHOCOLATE
COATING**

150g tempered dark
  chocolate, 70% cocoa solids
  (page 34)

These madeleines use the classic batter from Tier 1 (page 92), but by adding a small amount of cocoa powder, we'll create an eye-catching striped design. It's important to bake these in a silicone madeleine mold as we'll add tempered chocolate to create the shiny shell on the outside.

1. Use a knife to cut down the center of the vanilla bean pod and then scrape out the seeds into a small saucepan.

2. Place the saucepan on the stovetop over medium heat. Add the butter and stir until melted. Remove the saucepan from the heat and allow the mixture to cool.

3. In a medium bowl, whisk together the sugar and baking powder. Add the eggs and whisk until everything is combined.

4. Sift the flour into the bowl and whisk everything together until smooth.

5. Whisk in the vanilla and butter mixture. Mix until everything is fully incorporated and combined.

6. In a medium bowl, combine 120 grams of the batter and the cocoa powder. Stir until the cocoa powder is completely incorporated. Cover both bowls with plastic wrap/cling film and refrigerate overnight.

7. Preheat the oven to 465°F/240°C. Remove the bowls from the fridge and leave them at room temperature for 10 minutes to soften slightly.

8. Lightly grease the cups of a silicone madeleine mold with softened butter and gently sift a little flour into each cup. Tap the mold to remove any excess flour.

9. Add each batter to a piping bag, but snip a smaller hole for the chocolate batter bag. Fill each cup two-thirds full with the vanilla batter. Pipe thin stripes over the top with the chocolate batter, varying the lengths of the stripes.

10. Place the mold in the oven and immediately drop the temperature to 355°F/180°C. Bake the madeleines for about 10–11 minutes or until they're lightly golden around the edges and they have a nice hump in the center.

11. Remove the pan from the oven and allow the madeleines to cool for a few minutes before carefully popping them out of the silicone mold.

12. Allow the madeleines to cool for 15 minutes more. Completely clean the madeleine mold while the madeleines cool.

13. Add the tempered dark chocolate to a piping bag and fill one madeleine cavity about ⅓ full. Working quickly, press one madeleine "shell side" down into the tempered chocolate. The chocolate should squish up around the madeleine—just to the lip of the pan. Adjust the amount of chocolate you pipe depending on how the first one went and repeat this process with the remaining madeleines. It is important to do this in a silicone madeleine mold, as the chocolate will stick to metal.

14. Allow the madeleines to sit in the mold for 10 minutes, or until the chocolate has fully set. Carefully pop out the madeleines before serving.

Strawberry and Almond Tart

MAKES 1 TART

FOR THE PASTRY

1 batch Vanilla Pastry
  (page 28)

FOR THE ALMOND CREAM

100g unsalted butter,
  softened

100g powdered/icing sugar

75g eggs

½ tsp pure almond extract
  (optional)

12g cornstarch/corn flour

100g ground almonds

Strawberry jam

500g strawberries (about
  2 pints/punnets)

Lemon thyme, for finishing

SPECIAL EQUIPMENT

9-inch (23cm) fluted
  tart pan/tin with a
  removable base

Stand mixer, with the
  paddle attachment

Piping bag, plus a
  (0.5 inch/15mm)
  round tip nozzle

Fresh strawberries in-season are easily my favorite fruit for desserts. The pop of color and sweetness they bring to a dish is perfect for summer. Using an almond cream in the base of the tart is a classic French pastry technique, and also means we don't need to blind-bake it. For some added texture, try adding toasted, flaked almonds on top of the almond cream before you bake it.

1. Prepare the Vanilla Pastry for the 9-inch × 23cm fluted tart pan with a removable base. You are not going to blind-bake the pastry, so once you have lined the tart pan with the pastry, refrigerate it on a tray until you have made the almond cream. Preheat the oven to 345°F/175°C.

2. To make the almond cream, to the bowl of a stand mixer fitted with the paddle attachment, add the butter. Sift in the sugar and beat on medium speed for 2–3 minutes or until smooth and slightly lighter in consistency.

3. With the mixer still running, very slowly add the eggs and almond extract. Scrape down the bowl and mix again. Don't worry if the eggs don't look like they've been fully incorporated.

4. Add the cornstarch/corn flour and ground almonds and beat until there are no more dry bits.

5. Add the cream to a piping bag fitted with a large round nozzle and remove the pastry case from the fridge. Pipe an even layer of the cream into the tart shell, filling it up about halfway.

6. Slice 3–4 of the strawberries and press the slices into the top of the almond cream.

7. Place the tart into the oven and bake for 30–35 minutes, or until the almond cream has a golden color.

8. Remove the tart from the oven and allow to cool at room temperature for 30 minutes.

9. Spread a few dollops of strawberry jam in a thin layer across the top of the baked tart. Just add a thin layer to ensure that the tart doesn't become too sweet.

10. Slice the remaining strawberries and place them all over the tart, along with some lemon thyme for a pop of color. To add some variety in the texture, slice the strawberries horizontally and vertically. This is best served on the same day while the strawberries are fresh.

Raspberry and Pistachio Tartlets

MAKES 6 TARTLETS

FOR THE COMPOTE

20g granulated/caster
  sugar, divided

3g pectin NH powder

200g raspberries

10g fresh lemon juice

FOR THE PASTRY

1 batch Vanilla Pastry
  (page 28)

**FOR THE PISTACHIO
CREAM**

100g unsalted butter,
  softened

100g powdered/icing sugar

75g eggs

12g cornstarch/corn flour

50g ground almonds

50g ground pistachios

**FOR THE MASCARPONE
CREAM**

250g heavy/double cream

5g powdered/icing sugar

50g mascarpone

½ tsp vanilla bean paste

Raspberries, for decorating

Powdered/icing sugar,
  for decorating

Crushed pistachios,
  for decorating

This tart is the epitome of desserts I love to make—bursting with flavors and textures. It starts with the same pastry and filling as the Tier 1 tart (page 99), but we're using pistachios instead of almonds. Then it's layered with a fresh raspberry compote, mascarpone cream and crushed pistachios.

1. To make the raspberry compote, in a small bowl, combine 10g of the granulated/caster sugar and the pectin. Mix until thoroughly combined and set aside.

2. In a medium saucepan over medium heat, combine the raspberries, lemon juice, and the remaining 10g of sugar. Stir until the raspberries start to break down and the mixture is bubbling, about 3 minutes. Add the pectin mixture and cook for 1 minute more.

3. Remove the saucepan from the heat and pour the mixture into a small bowl. Cover the surface with plastic wrap/cling film and refrigerate until needed.

4. Prepare the Vanilla Pastry for six 3 × 0.8 inch (7.6 × 2cm) perforated tart rings (see page 33). You are not going to blind-bake the pastry however, so once you have lined the rings, refrigerate them on a tray until you have made the pistachio cream. Preheat the oven to 345°F/175°C.

5. To make the pistachio cream, in the bowl of a stand mixer fitted with the paddle attachment, combine the butter and sugar. Beat on medium for 2 minutes or until the mixture is smooth, pausing to scrape down the sides as needed.

6. With the mixer still running, slowly add the eggs in stages. Once you've added all the eggs, scrape down the bowl and mix for 1 minute more. Don't worry if they don't look like they've fully incorporated.

7. Add the cornstarch, ground almonds, and ground pistachios. Beat until everything is fully incorporated. Add the mixture to a piping bag.

8. Remove the chilled tart shells from the fridge. Use scissors to snip off roughly ½ inch (1.3cm) from the end of the piping bag. Pipe the cream into the base of the tartlet shells, filling them just below halfway.

9. Place the baking tray in the oven and bake the tartlets for about 15–20 minutes or until the cream has a light golden color on top.

10. Remove the tray from the oven and allow the tartlets to cool for 5 minutes before carefully removing the tart rings.

6× 3 (W) × 0.8-inch (H)
(7.6 × 2cm) perforated
tart rings

Stand mixer, with the paddle
attachment and the whisk
attachment

2× piping bags, plus a (0.5
inch/15mm) round tip
nozzle

11. Prepare the egg wash. Use a pastry brush to brush a thin layer of egg wash on the edges of the tartlet shells.

12. Place the tray back in the oven and bake the tarts for 5–7 minutes more, or until the pastry is a nice golden color. Remove the tray from the oven and allow the tarts to cool to room temperature.

13. Remove the raspberry compote from the fridge and stir just to slightly loosen it. Scoop some of the compote into the center of each baked tart and use a palette knife to smooth it so it's flush with the tart edge.

14. To make the mascarpone cream, in the bowl of a stand mixer fitted with the whisk attachment, combine the cream, sugar, mascarpone, and vanilla bean paste. Whisk on medium until medium soft peaks form, being careful not to over-whip.

15. Add the cream into a piping bag fitted with a large round-tip piping nozzle.

16. Pipe a large dollop of the cream into the center of a tartlet, so it covers roughly ⅔ of the tartlet. Then firmly tap the tartlet against the work surface, this will flatten the cream and spread it just to the edge of the tartlet.

17. Place a few fresh raspberries on the cream, then dust lightly with powdered sugar. Finally, sprinkle crushed pistachios over the top.

18. Repeat with the remaining tartlets. These are best served the same day.

Blueberry and Mascarpone Choux Buns

MAKES 20 CHOUX BUNS

FOR THE MASCARPONE CREAM

3g powdered gelatin

18g cold water

100g mascarpone

10g powdered/icing sugar, plus extra to decorate

300g heavy/double cream

½ tsp vanilla bean paste

FOR THE BLUEBERRY COMPOTE

250g blueberries, divided

2g cornstarch/corn flour

5g granulated/caster sugar

30–60g water

2g lemon zest

FOR THE CRAQUELIN

60g unsalted butter, softened

65g light brown sugar

65g all-purpose/plain flour

35g ground almonds

FOR THE CHOUX PASTRY

Nonstick cooking spray

90g water

80g whole milk

85g unsalted butter, cubed

5g granulated/caster sugar

2.5g sea salt

85g bread/white bread flour

155g eggs

I can't begin to count the number of times my choux buns failed when I first started baking. Too often my choux would be misshapen or burst in the oven, but the secret I was missing was craquelin. It's a crunchy, sugary dough that sits on top of your choux pastry, and acts as the perfect little umbrella to keep your buns in order. It melts over the top to not only add a great texture, but to maintain a uniform shape, and avoid the disappointment of those misshapen choux!

1. To make the mascarpone cream, in a small bowl, combine the gelatin and cold water. Stir and allow the mixture to bloom for 5 minutes.

2. In a tall jug/cup, combine the mascarpone and sugar. Set aside.

3. In a medium saucepan on the stovetop over medium heat, combine the cream and vanilla bean paste. As soon as the mixture is steaming but not boiling, remove the saucepan from the heat and stir in the bloomed gelatin until it has completely dissolved.

4. Pour the cream mixture into the jug and blend with a hand blender until smooth. Transfer the mixture to a large bowl. Cover the surface with plastic wrap/cling film and refrigerate for at least 6 hours, or ideally overnight.

5. To make the compote, in a medium saucepan on the stovetop over medium heat, combine 170g blueberries, the cornstarch, sugar, water, and lemon zest. Stir until the blueberries have broken down and the sauce has slightly thickened. Start with 30g of water, then add more as needed if the mixture looks too dry.

6. Remove the saucepan from the heat and stir in the remaining 80g of blueberries. Transfer the mixture to a large bowl and refrigerate until needed.

7. To make the craquelin, in the bowl of a stand mixer fitted with the paddle attachment, combine the butter and brown sugar. Beat the mixture for 2 minutes or until smooth, scraping down the bowl as needed.

8. Add the flour and ground almonds. Mix on low speed until the ingredients pull together into a dough.

9. Take two large pieces of parchment paper and scoop the dough into the center of one. Place the second sheet of parchment on top and use a rolling pin to roll the dough into a rough circle, about 0.2 inches (0.5cm) thick. Freeze the dough for 20 minutes.

Hand blender

Stand mixer, with
the paddle attachment
and the whisk attachment

Rolling pin

4× baking trays/sheets

Instant read thermometer

2× piping bags, plus 1 round
tip nozzle and 1 large open
star tip nozzle

10. Remove the dough from the freezer. Working quickly, peel off the top sheet of parchment paper and cut the dough into disks about 2 inches (5cm) in diameter. Place these on a baking tray lined with parchment paper and place the tray in the freezer. You'll need around 20 disks, so if you don't have enough, simply re-roll the dough, freeze it again, and cut the remaining needed disks.

11. To make the choux pastry, you need to have your mise en place, or set-up, ready before starting or else you'll get yourself into a tangle of stress. You should:

- Weigh the flour.
- Weigh and thoroughly whisk the eggs, then add them to a jug.
- Set up your stand mixer with the paddle attachment.
- Add a 0.5-inch (13mm) round nozzle to a piping bag.
- Preheat the oven to 355°F/180°C. Place a small baking tray at the very bottom of the oven.

12. On two large pieces of parchment paper, draw 10 circles that are evenly spaced and 1.9 inches (4.8cm) in diameter on each. These are guides for how large to pipe each choux so they're even. Spray two baking trays with nonstick cooking spray and press the parchment paper ink-side down onto the trays. Set aside.

13. In a medium saucepan on the stovetop over medium heat, combine the water, milk, butter, sugar, and salt. Bring the mixture to a boil, stirring occasionally. Immediately remove the saucepan from the heat and sieve the flour over the top. (Always sieve the flour or you could get lumps.)

14. Stir the mixture off the heat with a spatula until the flour is fully incorporated, then place the saucepan back on the heat. Stir the mixture constantly for 2 minutes, by which point a thin film of dough should form on the bottom of the pan and the dough should look shiny.

15. Immediately remove the saucepan from the heat and transfer the mixture into the bowl of the stand mixer. Beat on a medium-low speed until the mixture has cooled to 122–140°F/50–60°C.

16. Start adding the eggs. You want to add them in 6 parts, so add them in slowly, ensure they fully incorporate, and wait about 30 seconds before you add the next part. Take your time here because you want to ensure the eggs are properly absorbed. You may not need all of the egg mixture—you are looking for a choux pastry that is glossy and holds a ribbon when you drizzle it from the beater.

17. Once you have the right consistency keep mixing the dough on a low speed for about 2–3 minutes to allow the dough to cool, then transfer the dough to a piping bag.

18. Use your hand to press the choux pastry up the piping bag, flatten it with your hand, and press it back down into the base of the piping bag. This will remove any air bubbles as you pipe.

19. Applying even pressure and holding the piping bag vertically, pipe dollops of the choux pastry just inside the lines you drew on the parchment paper. (Don't go right to the line because the craquelin needs to cover the choux.)

20. Remove the craquelin discs from the freezer and quickly place them into the center of each choux.

21. Open the oven, splash a very small amount of water onto the tray at the bottom, and place the trays in the oven. Don't open the oven during baking or you'll lose the steam. Bake for around 30–35 minutes, or until the choux are a nice golden color. Remove the trays from the oven and allow them to cool .

22. Use a serrated knife to carefully slice a little lid off the top of each choux. Add a few spoonfuls of the chilled blueberry compote into the hollow of each choux.

23. Remove the mascarpone cream from the fridge and add it to the bowl of a stand mixer fitted with a whisk attachment. Whisk the mixture for 2–3 minutes, or until it has a medium-stiff peak. Be careful not to over-whisk.

24. Add the cream to a piping bag fitted with a large open star tip nozzle. Holding the piping bag vertically, apply even pressure and pipe a kiss shape on the top of a choux. Repeat this for the remaining choux buns then serve.

Pistachio Paris-Brest

MAKES 8 PARIS-BREST

FOR THE PISTACHIO CRÉMEUX

6g powdered gelatin

36g cold water

270g white chocolate, chopped

135g pistachio paste

1080g heavy/double cream, divided, cold

FOR THE CRAQUELIN

80g unsalted butter, softened

85g light brown sugar

85g all-purpose/plain flour

45g ground almonds

FOR THE CHOUX

90g water

80g whole milk

85g unsalted butter, cubed

5g granulated/caster sugar

2.5g sea salt

85g bread/white bread flour

155g eggs

Roughly chopped pistachios, for topping

1 batch Pistachio Praline Paste (page 225), for topping

Powdered/icing sugar, for topping

Creating uniform, professional-looking choux pastry is always a challenge as a home baker, but the secret is silicone molds. Here we are using the same recipe as in Tier 1 (page 104), but by piping the choux pastry and freezing it in a silicone donut mold, it ensures we get perfect consistency every single time. The pistachio crémeux is a decadent texture and the beautiful bright green pops of pistachio make this an eye-catching pastry.

1. To make the pistachio crémeux, in a small bowl, stir together the powdered gelatin and cold water. Allow it to sit for 5 minutes.

2. In a large bowl, combine the pistachio paste and chopped white chocolate. Set aside.

3. Add 280g of cream to a medium saucepan over medium heat. Stir until the cream is steaming, but not boiling. Remove the saucepan from the heat and stir in the bloomed gelatin until it dissolves.

4. Pour the hot cream over the pistachio mixture, let it sit for 2 minutes and then use a hand blender to blend until smooth. Add the remaining 800g of cold cream and blend again. Cover the surface with plastic wrap/cling film and refrigerate overnight.

5. To make the craquelin, in the bowl of a stand mixer fitted with the paddle attachment, combine the butter and brown sugar. Mix on a medium speed until smooth, about 1–2 minutes, pausing to scrape down the sides of the bowl as needed.

6. Add the flour and ground almonds. Mix on low until the mixture forms a dough.

7. Place the craquelin on a large silicone mat and place a second silicone mat on top of the dough. Use a rolling pin to roll the dough into a rough rectangle, about 0.2 inches (5mm) thick. Freeze the dough for 20 minutes.

8. Remove the craquelin from the freezer and allow the dough to sit for 1 minute at room temperature.

9. Working quickly, peel off the top silicone mat and use a 3-inch (8cm) cookie cutter to cut the dough into 8 disks. Use the round base of a 0.6-inch (1.5cm) piping nozzle to cut a small hole from the center of each disk. Place the discs on a baking tray lined with a silicone mat and freeze until ready to use. If the dough becomes too soft while cutting, refreeze for 5 minutes and then carry on.

SPECIAL EQUIPMENT

Hand blender

Stand mixer, with the
paddle attachment
and whisk attachment

Rolling pin

2× silicone mats

3-inch (8cm) cookie cutter

0.7-inch (1.8cm) round
tip nozzle

2 baking trays/sheets

Instant read thermometer

2× piping bags, plus a 0.6-inch
(1.5cm) round tip nozzle and
a star tip (4B)

Silicone donut mold

10. To make the choux, in a medium saucepan over medium heat, combine the water, milk, butter, sugar, and salt. Bring to a boil, then immediately remove the saucepan from the heat. Sift in the flour and gently stir until there are no more dry bits.

11. Return the saucepan to the heat and stir the mixture constantly for 2 minutes, or until a thin film of dough forms on the bottom of the pan and the dough looks shiny.

12. Transfer the dough to the bowl of a stand mixer fitted with the paddle attachment and mix on medium-low until the dough has cooled to 122–140°F/ 50–60°C.

13. With the mixer on medium, slowly start adding the eggs, in about 6 parts, allowing each addition of egg to mix for about 30 seconds before adding the next. You might not need all the egg mixture. You're looking for a choux pastry that's glossy and holds a ribbon when you drizzle it from the beater.

14. Once you've added all the eggs, begin to mix on medium-low for 2–3 minutes to allow the pastry to cool. Transfer the dough to a piping bag fitted with 0.6-inch (1.5cm) round tip nozzle.

15. Fill 8 silicone donut mold cavities (about 2.5 inches [6.5cm] each) piping about 35g of choux. Freeze the mold for 3 hours.

16. Preheat the oven to 355°F/180°C. Place a small baking tray on the lower rack. Line a perforated baking tray with a perforated baking mat.

17. Pop the frozen choux from the molds and place them on the baking mat. Leave about 2.5 inches (6.5cm) between each choux as they'll puff up as they bake. If you can't fit them all on the mat, bake the choux in two separate batches.

18. Remove the craquelin disks from the freezer and carefully center them on the top of the choux.

19. Open the oven and splash about ½ cup of water on the hot tray. Immediately place the baking tray on the center rack. Bake for about 35 minutes or until they're a deep golden color. Resist the temptation to open the oven door. If you open the oven too early, the choux could collapse.

20. Remove the tray from the oven and allow the choux to cool for 1 hour.

21. Use a serrated knife to cut the choux in half horizontally. Take the top lid of the choux, and use a cookie cutter just slightly smaller in diameter, and cut a neat disk. This tidies up the edges and gives the Paris-Brest a clean look. (You can also cut a small hole for the center too.)

22. Place the 8 bottom choux halves on a serving platter. Sprinkle an equal amount of chopped pistachios on each. Drizzle a little Pistachio Praline Paste over the top.

23. Remove the pistachio crémeux from the fridge and add it to a stand mixer fitted with a whisk attachment. Whisk on a medium speed until it reaches a medium-stiff peak. Add it to a piping bag fitted with a star tip (4B) and pipe tight spirals on top of the praline.

24. Dust a small amount of powdered sugar over the top of the lid of each choux, then drizzle a circle of Pistachio Praline Paste. Attach a few chopped pistachios to the praline and then place the lids on top of the pistachio cream spirals.

Roasted Strawberry Crème Brûlée

**MAKES 4 CRÈME
BRÛLÉES**

**FOR THE ROASTED
STRAWBERRIES**
400g strawberries, halved
15g granulated/caster sugar

FOR THE CRÈME BRÛLÉE
1 fresh vanilla bean
100g whole milk
400g heavy/double cream
70g granulated/caster sugar
55g eggs
85g egg yolks

Powdered/icing sugar,
  for topping

SPECIAL EQUIPMENT
Baking tray/sheet
4× shallow crème brûlée
  ramekins
Blowtorch
Deep roasting tray

As simple as it is, vanilla is one of my favorite flavors, and crème brûlée is the perfect dessert to highlight this. The roasted strawberries act as a hidden little surprise when you crack into the crème brûlée.

1. Preheat the oven to 340°F/170°C.

2. To make the roasted strawberries, place the strawberries on a baking tray lined with parchment paper. Sprinkle the sugar over the top and gently work it into the strawberries with your fingertips.

3. Place the tray in the oven and roast the strawberries for 25–30 minutes, or until they're soft and juicy. Be careful not to burn them. Remove the tray from the oven and transfer the strawberries to a large bowl to cool.

4. To make the crème brûlée, cut the vanilla bean lengthwise and scrape the seeds from the center into a small dish.

5. In a medium saucepan on the stovetop over medium heat, combine the milk, cream, and vanilla bean. Stir until the mixture is steaming but not boiling. Turn off the heat, cover, and set aside for 30 minutes.

6. In a medium bowl, whisk together the sugar, eggs, and egg yolks. Whisk until just combined. Avoid adding too much air into the mixture.

7. Stir the cream mixture to disperse the vanilla. Slowly pour the warm cream over the egg mixture and stir with a spatula to combine.

8. Place a few slices of strawberries into the crème brûlée ramekins. (Try not to add the juices). Pour the crème brûlée mixture over the top, filling the ramekins to just below the rim. Use a spoon to skim off any foam and use a blow torch to gently eliminate any bubbles.

9. Place the ramekins in a deep roasting tray and fill the tray with boiling water until it reaches halfway up the sides of the ramekins.

10. Place the tray in the oven and bake the crème brûlée for 30–40 minutes, or until you see a very small wobble in the center of each crème brûlée.

11. Remove the tray from the oven and remove the ramekins from the water bath. Allow them to cool to room temperature and then refrigerate uncovered for a minimum of 3–4 hours.

12. Use paper towels to mop up any moisture on the top. Dust the surface with an even layer of powdered sugar and then use a blowtorch to melt it.

13. Add a second layer of powdered sugar and use the blow torch until the sugar has a deep caramel color. Serve immediately.

Cardamom and Orange Custard Tart

MAKES 1 TART

FOR THE PASTRY

1 batch Vanilla Pastry
  (Page 28)

**FOR THE CARDAMOM AND
ORANGE CUSTARD**

5 cardamom pods

8g orange zest

500g heavy/double cream

125g whole milk

180g egg yolks

90g granulated/caster sugar

SPECIAL EQUIPMENT

9-inch (23cm) fluted
  tart pan/tin with a
  removable base

Pestle and mortar

Baking tray/sheet

Blowtorch

Cardamom has always been a flavor I was afraid to use in baking, but paired with the orange citrus, it gives the tart a lovely fragrant hit as you bite into it. A custard tart is really just a fancy version of a crème brûlée, but in a tart shell. Once you've mastered the crème brûlée, we'll use the exact same technique to create the custard tart filling, adding the flavor infusions and baking it inside a sweet pastry case.

1. Prepare the vanilla pastry in a 9-inch (23cm) fluted tart pan with a removable base. Blind bake and egg wash it until golden then set it aside while you prepare the filling. Lower the oven temperature to 265°F/130°C.

2. Add the cardamom pods to a frying pan and toast for 2–3 minutes over medium heat, until they are toasty and fragrant. Use a pestle and mortar and crush them into a rough powder.

3. Add the powder to a medium saucepan along with the orange zest, cream and milk.

4. Gently cook the mixture over medium heat, stirring occasionally until the mixture is steaming. Once hot, turn off the heat, cover the pan and let it infuse for 30 minutes.

5. After 30 minutes, whisk the mixture to loosen it and bring it back to a gentle simmer.

6. While it heats up, add the egg yolks and sugar to a bowl and whisk for 2 minutes until they become thicker and paler in consistency.

7. Remove the hot cream from the heat and slowly pour it in 3 batches through a fine-mesh sieve, over the egg mixture, stirring gently with a spatula. Avoid using a whisk here as we don't want to add too many air bubbles into the batter. Use a spoon to scoop off any foam or bubbles that might be sitting on the surface.

8. Place the tart shell, still in the pan, in the center of the oven on a baking tray, and carefully pour the filling in, right to the top of the pastry. Use a blowtorch to gently torch any air bubbles on the surface. Bake for 45–50 minutes, or until there is a slight wobble in the center. Remove it from the oven, and allow to cool to room temperature before serving.

Blueberry "Pumble"

MAKES 1 PIE

FOR THE PIE DOUGH

250g cake/pastry flour, plus more for dusting

3g sea salt

10g granulated/caster sugar

205g unsalted butter, cold and cubed

65–80g ice-cold water

FOR THE FILLING

45g granulated/caster sugar

10g cornstarch/corn flour

20g all-purpose/plain flour

700g blueberries

50g water

7g fresh lemon juice

2g lemon zest

Pinch of ground cinnamon

FOR THE CRUMBLE

60g unsalted butter, cold and cubed

60g granulated/caster sugar

60g all-purpose/plain flour

30g ground almonds

30g jumbo rolled oats

Vanilla Bean Ice Cream, to serve (page 148)

Is it a pie? Is it a crumble? It's a pumble! I'm not sure I can quite say I created it, but when you want the best of both worlds, this pumble gives you a flaky pastry base bursting with a blueberry filling, then topped with a crunchy oat crumble. Although it takes some time, laminating the pie dough is going to give us all those buttery layers, and is by far the best way to make pie dough. Serve it warm with a scoop of Vanilla Bean Ice Cream (page 148) and watch it melt into the middle.

1. To make the pie dough, in a large bowl, combine the cake flour, salt, and sugar. Add the butter and use your hands to gently work the butter into the dry ingredients, squeezing it between your fingertips. Keep working it until the butter pieces have broken down to roughly the size of hazelnuts.

2. Adding just a tablespoon at a time, slowly add the ice-cold water, using your hands to toss the flour and incorporate the water. Keep adding the water, in small increments, until the dough pulls together when you squeeze it. You are looking for no more dry bits of flour. The amount of water you need to add will depend on the flour you are using, so keep a close eye on the consistency of the dough. Pull the dough together into a rough disc, wrap in plastic wrap/cling film and refrigerate for 30 minutes.

3. Remove the chilled dough from the fridge, and on a lightly floured surface, roll the dough into a rough rectangle shape, about 0.2–0.27 inch (5-7mm) thick. Brush off any excess flour and fold the dough into thirds, like you're folding a letter. If you find the dough is sticking at any point, use a floured bench scraper to get underneath the dough and loosen it.

4. Wrap the dough in plastic wrap, and chill it for 30 minutes. Once chilled, turn the dough so the open seam is facing you as you roll, and repeat this rolling and folding process (also known as laminating). Chill the dough once more, and perform one final lamination. You should have performed 3 folds in total.

5. Shape the dough into a rough block, then wrap it tightly in plastic wrap, and chill it for 30 minutes.

6. To make the blueberry filling, in a small bowl, whisk together the sugar, cornstarch, and all-purpose flour. Set aside.

7. In a medium saucepan on the stovetop over medium heat, combine the blueberries, water, lemon juice, zest, and cinnamon. Stir occasionally for 6–7 minutes or until the blueberries have started to break down and release their juices. Some whole blueberries should still remain.

SPECIAL EQUIPMENT

Rolling pin

Bench scraper

Small baking tray/sheet

9-inch (23cm) metal pie
  pan/tin

Baking tray/sheet

8. Stir in the sugar mixture and cook the mixture for 1–2 minutes more. Immediately pour the mixture on a small baking tray. Cover the surface with plastic wrap and refrigerate for about 30 minutes, or until completely cool to the touch.

9. To make the oat streusel, in a medium bowl, combine all the streusel ingredients. Rub the mixture between your fingers until the butter has broken down into small pieces and it resembles a crumble. Refrigerate the streusel until ready to use.

10. Remove the pie dough from the fridge and allow it to soften slightly so it's easier to roll. Flour the dough and your rolling pin, then roll the dough out, turning it 90° after every roll (keep flouring as needed). Once you have a rough circle that's about 0.2 inches (5mm) thick, lift the dough into a 9-inch (22.8cm) metal pie pan. Use a pair of scissors to trim the dough, so there is about ½ inch (1.27cm) of overhang.

11. Tuck the overhang of dough underneath itself to form a neat rim around the pan. Then, take your thumb and index finger on one hand and form a "V" shape. Place these on the edge of the rim of dough, and then press the index finger from your other hand through the "V" shape to create a crimp. Repeat this around the entire edge of the pie, then freeze the dough for 30 minutes.

12. Remove the filling and crumble from the fridge and the pie shell from the freezer. Scoop the filling into the shell and use the back of a spoon to spread it out evenly.

13. Sprinkle the streusel over the top, covering the entire pie so you can't see any filling. Refrigerate the pie for 30 minutes.

14. Preheat the oven to 410°F/210°C and place a baking tray on the bottom rack.

15. Place the pie in the oven on the tray and bake for 25 minutes.

16. Lower the temperature to 345°F/175°C and move the tray to the middle rack. Bake for 40 minutes more, or until the pie has a really deep golden color and the filling is bubbling up.

17. Remove the pie from the oven and allow to cool completely. Serve with Vanilla Bean Ice Cream.

Latticed Apple Pie

MAKES 1 PIE

FOR THE DOUGH

500g cake/pastry flour

6g sea salt

20g granulated/caster sugar

410g unsalted butter, very
    cold and cubed

130–160g ice-cold water

FOR THE FILLING

800g Braeburn apples
    (about 8)

15g fresh lemon juice

75g light brown sugar

15g granulated/caster sugar

18g cornstarch/corn flour

⅓ tsp ground cinnamon

1 tsp vanilla bean paste

freshly ground nutmeg

130g water

1 large egg, for egg wash

Turbinado/demerara sugar,
    for topping

Using the same laminated pie dough as Tier 1 (page 116), we are going to create a double-crust apple pie, but elevate the design by using a lattice cutter. This gives us a clean, consistent finish to the pie, as if it was straight out of a bakery. Alternatively, i'll show you how to make the lattice by hand in case you don't have a cutter. Cooking the apples before we add them to the pie means the filling is soft with all the hits of warming spices.

1. To make the dough, in a large bowl, combine the flour, salt, and sugar. Add the butter and use your hands to gently work the butter into the dry ingredients, squeezing it between your fingertips. Keep working it until the butter pieces have broken down to roughly the size of hazelnuts.

2. Slowly add the ice-cold water, just a tablespoon at a time, using your hands to incorporate the water. Keep adding the water, in small increments, until the dough pulls together when you squeeze it. You are looking for no more dry bits of flour. This is a larger quantity of dough compared to the Blueberry "Pumble" (Page 116), so it will take a little longer to pull together.

3. Transfer the dough to a lightly floured work surface and form it into a rough rectangle shape. Wrap in plastic wrap/cling film and refrigerate for 30 minutes.

4. Lightly flour the dough and use a rolling pin to roll the dough into a long rectangle, about 0.2–0.27 inch (5–7mm) thick. Brush off any excess flour and fold the dough into thirds, like you're folding a letter. If you find the dough is sticking at any point, use a floured bench scraper to get underneath the dough and loosen it. Wrap the dough in plastic wrap, and chill it for 30 minutes.

5. Transfer the chilled dough to a lightly floured work surface and turn the dough so the open seam is facing you as you roll. Repeat this rolling and folding process. Chill the dough once more and then perform one final lamination. You should have performed 3 set of folds in total.

6. Split the dough into two equal pieces and shape them into rough blocks, then wrap them tightly in plastic wrap, and chill for 30 minutes.

7. Split the chilled dough in half and keep one wrapped in the fridge while you roll the other. The dough might need a few minutes at room temperature to soften slightly before rolling. Roll the dough into a rough circle, about 0.2 inches (5mm) thick, flouring as needed. Remove one half of dough from the fridge, leaving it at room temperature for a few minutes to soften slightly before rolling. Roll the dough into a rough circle, about 0.2 inches (5mm) thick, flouring as needed.

SPECIAL EQUIPMENT

Stand mixer, with the
   paddle attachment

Rolling pin

Bench scraper

9-inch (23cm) metal pie
   pan/tin

Fluted pastry wheel

Lattice cutter

3× baking trays/sheets

8. Place the dough into a 9-inch (23cm) metal pie pan. Use your fingers to press the dough into the edges and then trim off any excess pastry. Refrigerate until ready to use.

9. With the remaining half of the dough, you have two design options, either creating a lattice by hand or by using a lattice cutter for a bakery-style finish.

10. To do it by hand, roll the remaining half of dough into a rectangle shape to the same thickness. Use a fluted pastry wheel to cut 11 long strips of dough, about 1.5-inches (4cm) wide. Place the strips on a baking tray and refrigerate until ready to use.

11. Alternatively, to use a lattice cutter, roll the dough into a rough circle, then lift it onto a baking tray and refrigerate it for 15 minutes. It is much easier to use a lattice cutter when the dough is chilled.

12. Transfer the chilled dough to your work surface and using a lattice cutter, press firmly into the dough. Peel off the cutter to reveal the pattern underneath. Carefully transfer the dough back to the tray and refrigerate until ready to use.

13. To make the filling, core and peel the apples. Cut the apples into small cubes, about 0.5 inches (1.3cm) and weigh the required amount.

14. In a large bowl, combine the apples and lemon juice, tossing to coat. (The lemon juice will prevent the apples from browning.) Add the sugar, cornstarch/corn flour, cinnamon, and vanilla bean paste. Grate a little nutmeg over the top. Mix well.

15. Transfer the apple mixture to a medium saucepan over medium heat. Add ⅓ of the water (about 40g) and cook until the apples have softened slightly, about 5 minutes, stirring as needed and adding more water so the mixture doesn't get too thick. You may not need all of the water.

16. Transfer the apple mixture to a baking tray and spread out the apples. Cover the surface with plastic wrap/cling film and refrigerate for 30 minutes, or until they're completely cool to the touch.

17. Remove the cooled apples and pie shell from the fridge and spread the apple filling on your chilled pie dough. Use the back of a spoon to flatten them evenly across the dough.

18. In a small bowl, whisk the egg and use a pastry brush to lightly glaze around the edge to act as a glue for the lattice strips.

19. If you are doing the lattice by hand, remove the strips from the fridge and allow them to sit at room temperature for a few minutes until they're flexible. Place 6 strips horizontally across the pie, spacing them out evenly. Starting from the left side of the pie, carefully fold back the 2nd, 4th, and 6th strips of dough, then place 1 strip vertically down the center of the pie. Unfold the horizontal strips back over.

20. Fold back the 1st, 3rd, and 5th strips, then leaving a little gap in between the strip you just added, place another strip vertically across the pie. Unfold the horizontal strips back over the top.

21. Repeat steps 19 and 20, working your way across the pie until you have completed the lattice. You should now have a total of 6 strips horizontally and 5 strips vertically.

22. Carefully trim any excess dough from the edges and use your thumb to gently press the strips against the egg-washed edge. Refrigerate the pie for 30 minutes.

23. If you're using the lattice cutter, remove the dough from the fridge and place it on top of the pie. Use your thumb to gently press the top against the egg-washed edge. Refrigerate the pie for 30 minutes.

24. Preheat the oven to 430°F/220°C. Place a baking tray on the lower rack.

25. Remove the pie from the fridge and use a pastry brush to brush a light egg wash all over the pastry. Sprinkle some turbinado sugar over the top.

26. Place the pie on the baking tray in the oven. Baking on the bottom shelf to begin will give you a nice golden base, so no soggy pastry. Bake for 25 minutes, then lower the oven temperature to 345°F/180°C. Move the tray to the middle shelf and continue to bake for 50 minutes more or until the pie has a deep golden color and the filling is bubbling up. Don't be afraid to really bake this to a deep color to ensure the base is properly cooked. If at any point you feel the pastry is browning too much, place a sheet of foil over the pie.

27. Remove the tray from the oven and allow the pie to cool at room temperature for at least 2 hours so the filling can set. This is best served slightly warm or at room temperature.

CHAPTER 5

cookies & ice cream

Muscovado-Dark Chocolate Chunk Cookies

MAKES 12 COOKIES

110g unsalted butter, softened

120g dark muscovado sugar

80g granulated/caster sugar

2g sea salt

50g eggs

225g all-purpose/plain flour

5g cornstarch/corn flour

5g baking soda

2g baking powder

180g chopped dark chocolate, 70% cocoa solids, plus more for topping

---

SPECIAL EQUIPMENT

Stand mixer, with the paddle attachment

3× baking trays/sheets

Cookie cutter

Every baker needs a classic chocolate chip cookie recipe. For me, I like them slightly crispy on the outside, with a soft and chewy center. By using muscovado sugar, we get more of that molasses flavor and the cookie retains more moisture, resulting in the perfect texture. I always use the best chocolate I can get my hands on for cookies, as it makes a huge difference in the flavor.

1. In the bowl of a stand mixer fitted with the paddle attachment, combine the butter, sugars, and salt. Beat on medium-high speed until the mixture is light and fluffy, about 3 minutes, pausing to scrape down the sides as needed.

2. Add the eggs and beat until they have been fully incorporated, scraping down the sides to make sure all the butter is also incorporated.

3. In a medium bowl, whisk together the flour, cornstarch, baking soda, and baking powder.

4. Place a sieve over the stand mixer bowl and sift the dry ingredients into the wet ingredients. Mix on low speed just until the flour has been incorporated.

5. Add the chopped dark chocolate and mix again to incorporate.

6. Roll the dough into 65g balls in your hand and place them on a baking tray. Cover with plastic wrap/cling film and refrigerate for 2 hours.

7. Preheat the oven to 340°F/170°C.

8. Working in batches, place 6 dough balls on a baking tray lined with parchment paper. Press a few more bits of chopped dark chocolate into the top of the balls.

9. Place the tray in the oven and bake for 12–14 minutes, or until lightly golden.

10. Remove the tray from the oven and, while still hot, take a cookie cutter slightly larger than the baked cookie and quickly rotate it around the cookie. This neatens up the edges and gives you a perfectly round cookie.

11. Allow the cookies to cool on the tray for 5 minutes before transferring them to a rack to cool completely.

TIER **ONE**

TWO
TIER

Toasted Milk Powder and Brown Butter Cookies

MAKES 12 COOKIES

150g unsalted butter

20g non-fat milk powder

120g dark muscovado sugar

80g granulated/caster sugar

2g sea salt

50g eggs

20g water

225g all-purpose/plain flour

5g cornstarch/corn flour

5g baking soda

2g baking powder

180g chopped dark chocolate, 70% cocoa solids, plus more for topping

Flaky sea salt

SPECIAL EQUIPMENT

2× baking trays/sheets

Stand mixer, with the paddle attachment

Silicone baking mat

If you love the flavor of brown butter then this cookie is for you. Taking the Tier 1 cookie recipe (page 126), we replace the butter with browned butter and double up the flavor by adding toasted milk powder to the dough. Milk powder is concentrated milk solids, which, when toasted, essentially act like a supercharged brown butter flavor for your cookie. It takes a little extra effort but is worth it for the end result.

1. Melt the butter in a medium saucepan over medium heat. Once the butter has melted, it will begin to bubble rapidly, then the bubbles will become much smaller and the pan will go very quiet. At this point, you're looking for a caramelized, nutty aroma coming from the pan. This should take about 3–4 minutes, but keep an eye on the butter so it doesn't burn.

2. Remove the saucepan from the heat and weigh 110g into a bowl. Refrigerate for 45 minutes or until the butter has a soft consistency, stirring occasionally.

3. Preheat the oven to 320°F/160°C.

4. Spread the milk powder on a baking tray and bake for 10–15 minutes until it has a golden brown color, stirring every few minutes. Remove the tray from the oven and set aside to cool completely.

5. In the bowl of a stand mixer fitted with the paddle attachment, combine the soft browned butter, the sugars, and salt. Beat on medium for 2–3 minutes, or until lighter in consistency, pausing to scrape down the sides of the bowl as needed.

6. Add the eggs and water (which makes up for the moisture lost when the butter is browned). Beat to combine, then scrape down the sides.

7. Sift the flour, cornstarch, baking soda, baking powder, and toasted milk powder into a medium bowl. Stir to fully combine, then add this mixture and the chopped dark chocolate to the stand mixer. Hold a little bit of the chocolate back as we will add some into the dough before baking. Mix on low just until it pulls together into a dough.

8. Divide the dough in half and transfer to two sheets of plastic wrap/cling film. Shape each half into a rough square shape, then wrap and refrigerate for 2 hours.

9. Preheat the oven to 340°F/170°C. Line a baking tray with a silicone baking mat.

10. Remove half the dough from the fridge and separate into six 65-gram chunks. Roll the dough between the palms of your hands to make smooth balls. Evenly space them on the baking tray. Take the remaining chopped chocolate and press a few chunks into the top of the dough balls.

11. Place the sheet in the oven and bake for 12–14 minutes. Remove the sheet from the oven and sprinkle sea salt flakes over the top. Allow the cookies to cool on the tray for a few minutes, then transfer them to a rack to cool completely before serving. Repeat with the remaining cookie dough.

All-Butter Shortbread

MAKES 14 COOKIES

125g unsalted butter,
  very soft

1.5g sea salt

1 fresh vanilla bean or 1 tsp
  vanilla bean paste

35g granulated/caster sugar,
  plus more for topping

150g all-purpose/plain flour

15g cornstarch/corn flour

SPECIAL EQUIPMENT

Stand mixer, with the
  paddle attachment

Rolling pin

2.6-inch (6.8cm) fluted
  cookie cutter

Baking tray/sheet

Silicone baking mat

My dad would serve shortbread as a petit four at the restaurant, making just enough to serve that evening's guests. I don't think I ever told him, but I would sneak into the pantry under the restaurant and steal a few shortbreads. These shortbreads remind me just of those, using corn starch (corn flour) so they melt in the mouth, and adding a final dusting of sugar once they come out of the oven for a sweet crunchy finish.

1. Preheat your oven to 320°F/160°C.

2. Add the butter and salt into the bowl of a stand mixer with the paddle attachment and beat for one minute on medium speed.

3. Cut the vanilla bean lengthways and scrape the seeds out. Add these into the bowl along with the sugar. Beat for 1–2 minutes on medium speed, pausing to scrape down the bowl as needed, until everything is combined.

4. In a separate bowl, whisk together the flour and cornstarch, then sift this over the stand mixer bowl.

5. Mix on low speed until it pulls together into a dough, ensuring any butter on the bottom has been fully incorporated.

6. Lift the dough into the center of a large piece of parchment paper and place a second sheet on top (or use 2 silicone mats). Use a rolling pin to roll out the dough to around 0.2 inch (0.5mm) thick. Place it in the fridge for 5–10 minutes, just until it's slightly firm.

7. Peel off the top piece of parchment paper or silicone mat, then use a 2.7 inch (6.8mm) fluted cookie cutter to quickly cut the cookies.

8. Lift the biscuits onto a baking tray lined with a silicone mat, then place the tray in the freezer for 15 minutes.

9. Remove the tray from the freezer and bake the shortbread for 15–20 minutes, or until they are lightly golden around the edges.

10. Remove the tray from the oven, and let them cool for a few minutes, before sprinkling some extra sugar on top of the shortbread.

11. Allow them to cool for 30 minutes before serving.

Pistachio and Orange Viennese Whirls

MAKES 18-20 COOKIES

215g unsalted butter,
  very soft

2.5g sea salt

80g powdered/icing sugar

2g orange zest

35g egg whites

240g all-purpose/plain flour

15g cornstarch/corn flour

200g dark chocolate, 70%
  cocoa solids, chopped

10g neutral/vegetable oil

Crushed pistachios,
  to decorate

SPECIAL EQUIPMENT

Stand mixer, with the
  paddle attachment

Baking tray/sheet

2× silicone baking mats

Piping bag with a 4B star tip
  nozzle

While the classic Tier 1 shortbread (page 130) is a little more rustic, these Viennese whirls level things up with the addition of egg whites in the dough. The dough is slightly stiffer, which means you are able to pipe them and create this stunning fluted design to the cookie. They are delicious on their own, but dipping in chocolate and coating in pistachio adds an elegant finish.

1. Preheat the oven to 320°F/160°C.

2. Into a stand mixer fitted with a paddle attachment, add the butter and salt. Beat it on medium speed for 1 minute.

3. Add in the sugar, along with the orange zest. Beat the mixture, pausing to scrape down the sides as needed, on a medium speed for 2 minutes.

4. Scrape down the bowl and pour in the egg whites. Mix it on medium speed. It won't pull together into a smooth mixture, so don't panic.

5. In a separate bowl, whisk together the flour and cornflour, then sift this over the stand mixer bowl.

6. Mix on low speed until it pulls together into a dough.

7. Add the dough into a piping bag fitted with a 4B star tip nozzle. If the dough is too cold it can be difficult to pipe, so use your hands to soften it inside the piping bag if needed.

8. Onto a baking tray lined with a silicone mat, pipe tight zigzag shapes, about 1.5 inches (3.8cm) in width.

9. Place the tray into the oven, and bake the biscuits for 25–30 minutes, or until they are lightly golden around the edges. Remove them from the oven and cool to room temperature.

10. Add the chocolate and oil to a medium bowl. Place this over a pot of gently simmering water on a medium heat, and continue to stir until completely melted. Pour this into a narrow container and let it cool for a few minutes.

11. Take a cooled biscuit and dunk one half into the chocolate. Let the excess drip off and place it onto a baking tray lined with a silicone mat.

12. Sprinkle crushed pistachio onto the chocolate edge and repeat for the remaining biscuits. Place the biscuits into the fridge for a few minutes to set the chocolate, then remove and serve at room temperature.

Peanut and White Chocolate Cookies

MAKES 10 COOKIES

110g unsalted butter, soft

85g light brown sugar

80g granulated/caster sugar

50g eggs

150g natural peanut butter, plus extra to decorate

150g all-purpose/plain flour

2.5g baking powder

pinch of flaky sea salt, plus extra to decorate

40g white chocolate chips

60g unsalted peanuts

SPECIAL EQUIPMENT

2× baking trays/sheets

Stand mixer, with the paddle attachment

Silicone baking mat

Cookie cutter

Because of the sweetness you get from white chocolate, peanut butter is the ideal flavor pairing, bringing a slight saltiness to the cookie that balances the whole thing. Here, small tricks, like creating a pool of peanut butter in the center along with roasted peanuts around the outside, are great ways to bring more textural elements to a simple cookie.

1. Preheat the oven to 345°F/175°C.

2. Add the peanuts to a small baking tray and roast them for 8–10 minutes, or until they are golden in color. Set them to one side to cool. Once cooled, chop 40g into small pieces, leaving the remaining nuts whole.

3. Add the butter and sugars into the bowl of a stand mixer fitted with a paddle attachment. Beat for 2 minutes until the mixture is light and fluffy, then slowly drizzle in the eggs, beating to combine.

4. Add in the peanut butter and beat again until it has been completely incorporated.

5. In a small bowl, whisk together the flour, baking powder, and salt. Sift this into the bowl of the stand mixer and mix on low speed, then add in the white chocolate chips and 40g of the chopped peanuts.

6. Mix just until a dough forms and there are no more dry bits left. Cover the surface with plastic wrap/cling film and refrigerate it for 15 minutes.

7. Use a spoon to scoop the dough into 60g portions (it will be quite soft) and shape those portions into balls.

8. Lift 5 pieces onto a baking tray lined with a silicon mat, evenly spaced, and then gently flatten the cookies so they are a puck shape. Bake them in the oven for 12–14 minutes, or until very lightly golden around the edges.

9. Once baked, remove them from the oven and while they are still warm, use a cookie cutter slightly larger than the cookie and perform quick circular motions around the outside to neaten it up. Then, take the back of a tablespoon measure and gently press this into the center.

10. Allow the cookies to cool for 30 minutes, meanwhile baking the remaining dough balls.

11. To decorate, spoon some extra peanut butter into the center of the cookie and add the remaining roasted peanuts around the outside. Finish with a pinch of flaky salt to balance the sweetness and serve.

Caramelized White Chocolate Cookies

MAKES 12 COOKIES

FOR THE CARAMELIZED WHITE CHOCOLATE

200g good-quality white chocolate, chopped

FOR THE COOKIE DOUGH

145g unsalted butter, softened

140g light brown sugar

100g granulated/caster sugar

85g egg

30g egg yolk

105g dark chocolate, 70% cocoa solids, melted and slightly cooled

280g all-purpose/plain flour

40g cocoa powder

4g baking powder

4g sea salt

SPECIAL EQUIPMENT

2× baking trays/sheets

Silicone baking mat

Stand mixer, with the paddle attachment

Cookie cutter

White chocolate is a classic cookie flavor that works perfectly in the Tier 1 cookies (page 134), but taking the extra step of caramelizing it completely changes the flavor profile. Although it's a slightly time-consuming process, it elevates the white chocolate giving it this toasty, golden flavor. Combined with the cocoa from the cookie dough, you not only get this eye-catching color contrast, but a rich, fudgy cookie with hits of those roasted white chocolate shards.

1. Preheat the oven to 250°F/120°C. Place the chopped white chocolate onto a baking tray lined with a silicone baking mat.

2. Place the tray into the oven and bake for 2 hours, stirring the chocolate with a spatula every 15 minutes, until it is a golden color. It will look quite dry and grainy for the first hour, but as you continue to cook, it will return to a melted chocolate consistency.

3. Once smooth and golden, remove it from the oven, spread it into a thin even layer and let it cool slightly. Place it into the freezer for 15 minutes ,or until it has set firm.

4. Break the chocolate into small shards then transfer to a bowl and set aside.

5. To make the cookies, add the softened butter and sugars to the bowl of a stand mixer. With the paddle attachment, beat it on medium speed for 2–3 minutes or until light and fluffy in consistency. Scrape down the sides as needed.

6. Slowly pour in the eggs and egg yolks, and beat again to combine.

7. Pour in the slightly cooled, melted chocolate and beat once more.

8. In a medium bowl, whisk together the remaining dry ingredients. Sift these into the bowl of the stand mixer and mix on a low speed until the dough just pulls together and there are no more dry bits remaining.

9. Add in 100g of the caramelized white chocolate shards. Briefly mix the dough one more time to combine.

10. Scoop the dough out onto a sheet of plastic wrap/clingfilm and shape it into a disk. Wrap it tightly and chill it in the fridge for 1 hour. Preheat the oven to 345°F/175°C.

11. Remove the chilled dough from the fridge and shape it into 65g balls.

12. Place 6 balls onto a baking tray, evenly spaced, and then take some remaining shards of caramelized white chocolate and press these into the outside of the dough ball.

13. Place them into the oven and bake for around 12 minutes. Remove them from the oven and, while they are still warm, take a cookie cutter that is slightly larger than the cookies, and quickly rotate it around the outside of each cookie to neaten it into a tight circle.

14. Allow the cookies to cool slightly before transferring them to a wire rack and bake the remaining dough. These are best served slightly warm.

Cappuccino Macarons

MAKES 15 MACARONS

FOR THE SHELLS

150g ground almonds

130g powdered/icing sugar

110g aged egg whites
  (see the tip)

1.5g cream of tartar

110g granulated/caster sugar

Q.S brown gel food coloring

FOR THE GANACHE

300g double/heavy cream

20g honey

2g good-quality instant coffee

270g dark chocolate, 70%
  cocoa solids, chopped

50g unsalted butter, softened

cocoa powder, for decorating

SPECIAL EQUIPMENT

Blender

Stand mixer, with the
  whisk attachment

2× piping bags, plus 2×
  0.3-inch (8mm) round
  nozzles

Silicone baking mat

Baking tray/sheet

Hand blender

Instant read thermometer

Conquering macarons is one of the greatest achievements as a home baker. When they rise with perfect little feet—there is no better feeling! To create these macarons, we are using a French meringue. French meringue is typically easier to make than other varieties, but, it's slightly more fragile compared to an Italian meringue, so be gentle when folding the batter. The ganache offers a rich, decadent pairing for the sweet macaron shell.

1. To make the macaron shells, in a blender, briefly pulse the ground almonds to create a fine powder. Be careful not to blend them for too long or you risk heating them and releasing the oils.

2. Sift the ground almonds through a sieve and weigh 135g. This will eliminate any big lumps of almonds and lead to a smooth shell. Transfer the ground almonds to a medium bowl.

3. Sift in the powdered sugar and stir with a spatula. Set aside.

4. In the bowl of a stand mixer fitted with the whisk attachment, combine the aged egg whites and the cream of tartar. Start by whisking on low speed for 3–5 minutes, or until the egg whites have lots of small bubbles over the surface and appear slightly frothy. It's really important to take your time here because you don't want big air bubbles in the meringue.

5. Once you have a nice layer of small bubbles, increase the speed to medium-high and slowly start adding the granulated sugar 1 tablespoon at a time. Allow the meringue to mix for about 20–30 seconds before adding the next tablespoon. Again, take your time here—you don't want to rush this process.

6. Once you've added all the sugar, add a drop of brown food coloring and keep whisking for 2 minutes more. Remove the bowl from the stand mixer. You should have a meringue that's stiff and glossy.

7. Use a spatula to gently fold half the almond mixture into the meringue. Once combined, add the remaining almond mixture and continue to fold gently. You want to loosen the mixture enough so the batter flows nicely off the spatula and forms a ribbon when you let it drizzle. You want that ribbon of batter to disappear into the remaining batter in about 10 seconds. It can take some practice (and some fails!) to really understand the correct consistency. If it's overmixed, it will be runny and spread too much as you pipe, but if it's undermixed, it will be too thick and will be difficult to pipe.

8. Transfer the mixture to a piping bag fitted with a 0.3-inch (8mm) round tip.

9. Place a silicone baking mat on a baking tray. Ensure the mat is very clean because any grease can affect the rise of the macarons.

10. Holding the piping bag vertically, apply even pressure and pipe a disk about 1.2 inches (3cm) wide. Once you've piped the disk, stop applying pressure and slowly whip the piping tip away in a circular motion.

11. Leave about a 1-inch (2.5cm) gap in between each shell and repeat the process. You should make roughly 30 shells.

12. Firmly tap the baking tray on your work surface a few times and then use a toothpick to carefully pop any air bubbles you see on the surface of the shells.

13. Use a small sieve to add a light dusting of cocoa powder around the outside of each shell. Allow the shells to rest for 20–30 minutes at room temperature. This helps to form a skin on the macaron shell.

14. Preheat the oven to 310°F/155°C. The macarons are ready for baking when the surface looks matte and the batter feels dry to the touch.

15. Place the tray on the middle rack in the oven and bake for 16–18 minutes. The macarons are done when you gently press one and it has a slight wobble.

16. Remove the tray from the oven and allow the macarons to cool at room temperature for 30 minutes before carefully peeling them off the mat. If they feel like they're sticking, place them in the freezer for 10 minutes, and they should pop right off.

17. You can fill the macaron shells straight away, but if you have the time, store them in an airtight container in the fridge overnight to mature them. This will allow the shells to absorb moisture and will result in a much better texture for your final product.

18. To make the coffee ganache, in a small saucepan on the stovetop over medium heat, combine the cream, honey, and instant coffee. Whisk to dissolve the coffee and the honey.

19. Add the chopped chocolate to a tall measuring jug/cup. Once the cream mixture is steaming but not boiling, pour it directly over the chocolate and allow the mixture to sit for 2 minutes.

20. Use a hand blender to blend the mixture until smooth. Add the butter and blend again. Pour the mixture into a medium bowl and cover the surface with plastic wrap/cling film. The ganache needs to cool at room temperature for about 2–3 hours, or until it has a thicker, more pipable consistency and reaches a temperature of about 77°F/25°C.

21. Add the ganache to a piping bag fitted with a round tip. On one macaron shell, pipe a dollop, leaving a small gap at the edges. Place another macaron shell atop the ganache, forming a sandwich, and apply enough pressure to press the ganache to the edge of the macaron shell. Repeat this step for all the shells to form 15 macarons. These are best kept at room temperature and served the same day to ensure the ganache stays soft.

Lemon Meringue Pie Macarons

MAKES 15 MACARONS

FOR THE MACARONS

175g ground almonds

150g powdered/icing sugar,
   plus more for topping

110g egg whites, divided

1 drop of yellow gel
   food coloring

1.5g cream of tartar

38g water

150g granulated/caster sugar

1 drop of pure lemon extract

FOR THE CRÉMEUX

150g granulated/caster sugar

8g lemon zest

240g eggs

110g fresh lemon juice

290g unsalted butter,
   softened

**FOR THE MERINGUE
STICKS**

70g egg whites

70g granulated/caster sugar

70g powdered/icing sugar

50g white chocolate, melted

While for the Tier 1 macarons (page 140) we used a French meringue, these lemon macarons increase the difficulty level by using an Italian meringue. It can be slightly more of a balancing act to get this meringue correct, but the final product is more stable than a French meringue, making the folding process easier. The meringue also gives you a smoother macaron shell with more shine. We elevate the design by adding a delicate meringue stick that gives them a professional touch.

1. To make the macaron shells, in a blender, briefly pulse the ground almonds to create a fine powder. Be careful not to blend them for too long or you risk heating them and releasing the oils.

2. Sift the ground almonds through a sieve and weigh 150g. This will eliminate any big lumps of almonds and lead to a smooth shell. Transfer the ground almonds to a medium bowl.

3. Sift the powdered sugar into the bowl. Stir well to combine.

4. Add 55g of egg whites and 1 drop of gel food coloring. Mix with a spatula until the mixture forms a thick sticky paste. Set aside.

5. In the bowl of a stand mixer fitted with the whisk attachment, combine the cream of tartar and the remaining 55 grams of egg whites. Whisk on medium-low speed. It's quite a small amount of egg whites, so the whisk might not quite catch them. If not, give them a quick whisk by hand to thicken them before placing the bowl back on the mixer.

6. In a small saucepan over medium heat, combine the water and granulated sugar. Heat the mixture to 244°F/118°C. At this point, the egg whites should be thick and frothy.

7. Immediately remove the sugar syrup from the heat, increase the mixer speed to medium-high, and slowly drizzle in the syrup between the whisk and the bowl. Whisk for 6–7 minutes, or until the bowl feels cool to the touch and the meringue has stiff peaks. Just before you stop whisking, add 1 drop of lemon extract.

8. Using a spatular, fold ⅓ of the meringue into the almond mixture. Initially, it will be quite stiff, but just keep mixing until the meringue is well incorporated. Fold in another ⅓ of meringue until evenly mixed. Add the remaining ⅓ of meringue. At this point, keep an eye on your mixing because you don't want to over-mix. You'll know it's ready when you can lift the spatula from the bowl and the batter drops from the spatula, forms a ribbon in the bowl, and then settles flat on itself within about 8–10 seconds.

SPECIAL EQUIPMENT

Blender

Stand mixer, with the
  whisk attachment

Hand blender

Instant read thermometer

3× Piping bag, plus a 0.3-inch
  (8mm) round tip nozzle,
  0.15-inch (4mm) round tip
  nozzle and 0.3-inch(8mm)
  round tip nozzle

2× baking trays/sheets

2× silicone baking mats

9. Add the batter to a piping bag fitted with a 0.3-inch (8mm) round tip nozzle. Line a baking tray with a silicone baking mat. Ensure the mat is very clean because any grease can affect the rise of the macarons. Holding the piping bag vertically, apply even pressure and pipe a disk about 1¼ inches (3cm) wide. Once you've piped the disk, stop applying pressure and slowly whip the piping nozzle away in a circular motion. Leave a 1-inch (2.5cm) gap between the shells. Pipe the remaining batter—you should create about 30 shells.

10. Tap the tray firmly on the work surface a few times, then use a toothpick to carefully pop any air bubbles you see on the surface of the shells. Allow the shells to rest at room temperature for 20–30 minutes or until they look matte and are no longer wet to the touch.

11. Preheat the oven to 310°F/155°C.

12. Place the tray on the center rack of the oven and bake the shells for 16–18 minutes or until they have a slight wobble when you touch them. Remove the tray from the oven and allow the shells to cool at room temperature for 30 minutes before carefully peeling them off the mat. If they feel like they're sticking, freeze them for 10 minutes and they should then pop right off. The macaron shells are best if you give them time to age by placing them in an airtight container and refrigerating them overnight. This will allow them to absorb some moisture and give you a softer macaron shell.

13. To make the lemon crémeux, in a medium bowl, combine the sugar and lemon zest. Rub these together with your fingertips, which will release the citrus oils, until it smells fragrant.

14. Add the eggs and lemon juice. Mix well to combine.

15. Place the bowl over a pan of gently simmering water. Whisk constantly until the mixture thickens and reaches a temperature of about 176°F/80°C.

16. Remove the bowl from the pan. Pass the mixture through a sieve and into a tall measuring jug/cup. Allow to cool to 140°F/60°C, stirring occasionally.

17. Use a hand blender to blend in the butter a piece at a time until you have a smooth mixture. Transfer the mixture to a large bowl and cover the surface with plastic wrap/cling film. Refrigerate for 1–2 hours, or until it's a more pipable consistency.

18. To make the meringue sticks, preheat the oven to 195°F/90°C.

19. To the bowl of a stand mixer fitted with the whisk attachment, add the egg whites and whisk on medium. Once the egg whites become thick and frothy, slowly start adding the granulated sugar about 1 tablespoon at a time, waiting 20 seconds before the next addition.

20. Once you've added all the sugar, whisk for 2 minutes more. The meringue should have a stiff peak and you shouldn't feel any sugar granules when you rub it between your fingertips.

21. Remove the bowl from the mixer and sift the powdered sugar into the bowl.

22. Fold this in gently with a spatula until it's all incorporated and the meringue is smooth. You'll have more meringue than you need, but you can use any extra to make little meringue kisses.

23. Add the meringue to a piping bag fitted with a 0.15-inch (4mm) round tip nozzle. Place a silicone mat on a baking tray and pipe long, thin lines of meringue the length of the mat.

24. Place the tray in the oven and bake the meringue for 90 minutes. Remove the tray from the oven and allow the meringue to cool to room temperature.

25. To assemble the macarons, remove the chilled lemon crémeux from the fridge and add it to a piping bag with a 0.3-inch (8mm) round tip nozzle. On half the macaron shells, pipe a dollop of the lemon crémeux—but not quite to the edges. Carefully place the remaining shells on top of the crémeux.

26. Carefully break the meringue into 3-inch-long (8cm) sticks. Use a pastry brush to brush a small amount of melted white chocolate on the bottom of a meringue stick. Carefully lay this on top of the macaron shell. Add some white chocolate to a second meringue stick and place this across the top to form an "X" shape. If you have chocolate cool spray, use this to quickly set the chocolate. Repeat with the remaining macarons. Finish the macarons with a dusting of powdered sugar. These are best served the same day because the meringue sticks will start to soften the longer they're left out.

Vanilla Bean Ice Cream

MAKES 1 BATCH

105g granulated/caster sugar

2g locust bean gum

2 fresh vanilla beans

550g whole milk

195g heavy/double cream (between 32–35% fat content)

55g glucose syrup

45g non-fat milk powder

45g egg yolks

SPECIAL EQUIPMENT

Instant read thermometer

Hand blender

Ice cream machine

Until I started developing this book, I didn't quite realize the intricacies of making great ice cream. Although there are some advanced ingredients in this recipe, these small additions make a huge difference to the overall flavor and texture by slowing the melting or reducing the size of ice crystals. Once you have confidence in making this recipe, you will have the fundamental knowledge to create a variety of flavors and can start to play around with fat or sugar levels to your preference.

1. In a small bowl, whisk together the sugar and locust bean gum. Whisk thoroughly and set aside.

2. Carefully cut the vanilla beans lengthwise. Use a knife to scrape the seeds from the center and add them to a medium saucepan.

3. Place the saucepan on the stovetop over medium heat. Add the milk, cream, glucose, and milk powder. Gently stir the mixture until it reaches 113°F/45°C.

4. Immediately add the sugar mixture, and egg yolks, and keep stirring until it reaches 185°F/85°C. This is an important temperature to reach to ensure the mixture has been properly pasteurized and the locust bean gum has fully hydrated.

5. Pour the mixture into a large bowl and use a hand blender to blend for 1 minute.

6. Place the bowl over a larger bowl of ice and stir, quickly cooling down the mixture to as close to 41°F/5°C as possible. This will take a few minutes, stirring occasionally, so stick with it! You might need to add more ice if it melts.

7. Cover the surface of the mixture with plastic wrap/cling film and refrigerate for 12 hours. This will age the ice cream base and help with the structure.

8. Remove the bowl from the fridge and use the hand blender to blend for 1 minute to slightly aerate the mixture.

9. Pour the mixture into an ice cream machine and churn. Depending on the machine, this will take about 30 minutes. It should look thick and creamy once ready.

10. Once the ice cream has been churned, you can eat it immediately, but it will be slightly soft. You can transfer the ice cream to an airtight container and freeze it for a few more hours until firmer.

Fresh Mint–Chocolate Chip Ice Cream

MAKES 1 BATCH

30g fresh mint leaves

105g granulated/caster
   sugar, divided

2g locust bean gum

550g whole milk

195g heavy/double cream
   (between 32–35%
   fat content)

55g glucose syrup

45g non-fat milk powder

45g egg yolks

Q.S green food color, powder
   (optional)

50g chocolate curls

SPECIAL EQUIPMENT

Rolling pin

Instant read thermometer

Hand blender

Ice cream machine

Mint chocolate chip is my go-to flavor, but fresh mint ice cream is a whole other experience. The brightness fresh mint brings is unrivaled and the process of turning the leaves into a paste is a really fun technique. The recipe is similar to the Tier 1 ice cream (page 148), with a few tweaks.

1. Pick the mint leaves, avoiding adding any with thick woody stems. Place the leaves on half of a large piece of parchment paper. Sprinkle 50g of sugar over the leaves and fold the parchment paper in half.

2. Use a rolling pin to roll back and forth over the mixture. Initially, it might be a little tricky to roll, but after a minute or two, the mixture should start to become wetter and eventually form a paste. Set aside in a small bowl.

3. In a separate small bowl, whisk together the locust bean gum and the remaining 55g of sugar. Mix until completely combined.

4. In a medium saucepan on the stovetop over medium heat, combine the milk, cream, glucose, and milk powder. Stir until the mixture reaches 113°F/45°C.

5. Add the sugar mixture and egg yolks. Continue to stir until the mixture reaches 185°F/85°C.

6. Remove the saucepan from the heat and add the mint paste. Stir for 1 minute, then use a hand blender to blend for about 30 seconds. Add the green food coloring powder (if using) and blend until you're happy with the color. (Achieving a bright green color by using fresh mint is tricky because of the heating process, which affects the chlorophyll in the leaves.)

7. Pour the mixture through a sieve and into a large bowl. Avoid pressing the sieve because you don't want to add any bitterness from the leaves.

8. Place the bowl over a larger bowl of ice and stir until the mixture has cooled to as close to 41°F/5°C as possible. Place a sheet of plastic wrap/cling film on the surface and refrigerate for 12 hours.

9. Blend the mixture once more to aerate, then pour it into your ice cream machine and churn. This will take about 30 minutes depending on your machine. The mixture should be thick and creamy.

10. Just before the ice cream is done, add the chocolate curls and mix until they're evenly incorporated.

11. You can eat the ice cream straight away, but it will be slightly soft. Otherwise, pour the ice cream into an airtight container and freeze for a few more hours until firmer.

TIER **ONE**

TWO
TIER

Ice Cream Sandwiches

**MAKES 6 ICE CREAM
SANDWICHES**

1 batch Vanilla Bean Ice
  Cream (or another flavor
  from the book)

FOR THE BISCUITS

55g granulated/caster sugar

110g unsalted butter,
  softened

150g all-purpose/plain flour

15g cocoa powder

Pinch of sea salt

Melted milk chocolate,
  for decorating

SPECIAL EQUIPMENT

2.7-inch (7cm) silicone
  disk mold

Stand mixer, with the
  paddle attachment

Rolling pin

Cookie cutter

Baking tray/sheet

Silicone baking mat

Piping bag

As a kid I would chase down the ice cream van in the summer, just to get my hands on that classic vanilla ice cream sandwich. This is a slightly fancier version, with a chocolate sable biscuit. The key to a perfect-looking ice cream sandwich is freezing the ice cream in a silicone mold, which gives you a really clean finish to the dessert.

1. Prepare the ice cream per the recipe.

2. Once the ice cream has been churned, scoop it into a 2.7-inch (7cm) silicone disk mold (typically, there are about 6 cavities in a silicone disk mold). Use a palette knife to smooth the tops, then place the molds into the freezer for 4–6 hours.

3. In a stand mixer, combine the sugar, butter, flour, cocoa powder, and salt. With the paddle attachment, mix on a medium-low speed until a crumbly dough forms and the butter has broken down into small pieces. Squeeze the dough between your hands to form a dough ball.

4. Transfer the dough to a large sheet of parchment paper. Place a second sheet of parchment paper on top of the dough. Use a rolling pin to roll the dough until it's quite thin, about 0.15 inches (4mm). (Don't worry too much about the shape of the dough because you'll be cutting it into disks.) Freeze the dough for 15 minutes.

5. Preheat the oven to 355°F/180°C.

6. Working quickly, peel off the parchment paper and use a cookie cutter to cut the dough into 2.7-inch (7cm) disks. You need 12 disks total, so re-roll any scraps of dough in case you don't cut enough.

7. Transfer the disks to a baking tray lined with a silicone baking mat and refrigerate the dough until ready to bake.

8. Place the tray in the oven and bake for 12 minutes. Remove the tray from the oven and gently flatten the cookies with a palette knife. Use the cookie cutter to trim the cookies so they are neat. Allow them to cool completely.

9. Add the melted milk chocolate to a piping bag. Cut a small hole from the tip and drizzle this over half the biscuits in a thin zigzag design.

10. Once the chocolate has set, pop the ice cream disks out of the silicone mold. Place each ice cream disk atop an undecorated biscuit and then place a decorated biscuit atop the ice cream. Allow the ice cream to soften slightly before serving.

Cookies and Cream Popsicles

MAKES 8 POPSICLES

40g Oreos, fillings removed

1 batch Vanilla Bean Ice Cream (page 148)

500g milk chocolate, 55% cocoa solids

65g cocoa butter (or grapeseed oil)

50g cocoa nibs

SPECIAL EQUIPMENT

8× silicone popsicle molds

8× popsicle sticks

It's hard not to love anything that has Oreos in it, and they pair perfectly with the Vanilla Bean Ice Cream recipe. As with the Tier 1 ice cream sandwiches (page 152), we are using a silicone mold to freeze the ice cream into a popsicle shape, but advancing it by dipping it in a smooth chocolate coating. The cocoa nibs add little bursts of bitterness to the sweet ice cream, but if you can't get hold of them, they can easily be replaced with chopped nuts or more chopped Oreos.

1. Into a sandwich bag, add the Oreo cookies and use a rolling pin to crush them.

2. Just before the ice cream is ready, add the crushed cookies and churn to incorporate them.

3. Work quickly to scoop the ice cream into 8 silicone popsicle molds and place the wooden popsicle sticks. Use a palette knife to completely smooth the top and freeze for 6 hours or overnight.

4. In a medium bowl, combine the milk chocolate, cocoa butter, and cocoa nibs. Place the bowl over a pan of gently simmering water. Stir constantly until everything has melted, then remove the bowl from the pan.

5. Allow the chocolate mixture to cool to about 104°F/40°C and then pour it into a tall, thin glass. You want a glass that's deep enough so you can dunk the entire popsicle in.

6. Pop the popsicles out of the mold and work quickly to dunk them into the chocolate coating. Dangle the popsicle over the glass until the excess coating stops dripping, then flip it upright and place it on a baking tray lined with a silicone mat.

7. Place the popsicles back in the freezer until ready to use or serve immediately.

Intense Chocolate Ice Cream

MAKES 1 BATCH

155g 70% dark chocolate,
  chopped
2g locust bean gum
50g granulated/caster sugar
650g whole milk
50g glucose syrup
40g dextrose powder
30g non-fat milk powder
15g cocoa powder

SPECIAL EQUIPMENT
Instant read thermometer
Hand blender
Ice cream machine

If you hadn't noticed already from this book—I'm a big chocolate lover and this ice cream is heaven. Using high-quality chocolate gives it intense cocoa notes with a smooth creamy texture. I dare you to try and resist taking a big scoop out of the machine when it finishes churning!

1. Place the chocolate in a medium bowl and set aside.

2. In a small bowl, combine the locust bean gum and sugar. Mix well and set aside.

3. In a medium saucepan on the stovetop over medium heat, whisk together the milk, glucose, dextrose, milk powder, and cocoa powder. Keep whisking until the mixture reaches 113°F/45°C on an instant-read thermometer.

4. Add the sugar and locust bean gum mixture. Continue to whisk until the temperature reaches 185°F/85°C. This is an important temperature to hit to ensure the mixture has correctly pasteurized and the locust bean gum has fully hydrated.

5. Remove the saucepan from the heat and pour the mixture over the chocolate. Use a hand blender to blend for 1 minute, then place the bowl over a larger bowl of ice. You need a lot of ice or this process will take some time. Keep stirring the chocolate mixture until cooled to as close to 41°F/5°C as possible.

6. Cover the bowl with plastic wrap/cling film and refrigerate for 12 hours.

7. Pour the mixture into an ice cream machine and churn. Depending on the machine, this might take around 30 minutes. It should look thick and creamy once ready.

8. Once the ice cream has been churned, you can eat it immediately, but it will be slightly soft. You can also transfer the ice cream to an airtight container and freeze for a few more hours until firmer.

Chocolate and Salted Caramel Sundae Pots

MAKES 6–8 POTS

1 batch of intense chocolate
  ice cream (page 156)

FOR THE CARAMEL SAUCE

45g whole milk

175g heavy/double cream

135g glucose syrup, divided

80g granulated/caster sugar

1.5g sea salt

60g unsalted butter

FOR THE COCOA CRUMBLE

60g cold unsalted butter,
  cubed

75g light brown sugar

75g all-purpose/plain flour

15g cocoa powder

1.5g sea salt

FOR THE CHANTILLY

400g heavy/double cream

10g granulated/caster sugar

½ fresh vanilla bean pod or
  1 tsp vanilla bean paste

While it's hard to beat chocolate ice cream on its own, this sundae is a great complement, with a dark chocolate crumble, whipped cream and oozing caramel. The crumble takes no time to pull together and can easily be prepared ahead of time and stored in the freezer—heated slightly before serving.

1. Preheat the oven to 320°F/160°C.

2. To make the salted caramel sauce, in a medium saucepan on the stovetop over medium heat, combine the milk, cream, and 45g of glucose. Bring to a gentle simmer, whisking to ensure the glucose has dissolved fully. Remove the saucepan from the heat, but ensure the mixture stays warm (gently re-heat, if necessary).

3. In a medium saucepan on the stovetop over medium heat, combine the sugar and the remaining 90g of glucose. Bring the mixture to a deep caramel. Try to avoid stirring the mixture and instead shake the pan to help disperse the sugar. If the sugar isn't breaking down, stir it very quickly with a spatula.

4. Once you have a deep golden color, immediately add the hot cream mixture, being very careful because it will bubble up violently. Whisk the mixture and cook for 1 minute.

5. Remove the saucepan from the heat and pour the mixture through a sieve into a large bowl. Allow the mixture to cool for 2 minutes, then add the salt and butter. Blend (or whisk) until smooth. Pour the mixture into a heatproof dish and let it cool to room temperature.

6. To make the cocoa crumble, in the bowl of a stand mixer with the paddle attachment, combine all the ingredients. Mix on low speed until it starts to form a crumble mixture. Squeeze the mixture with your hands to pull it together, then crumble it onto a baking tray.

7. Place the tray in the oven and bake for about 25 minutes, stirring the mixture 2–3 times to evenly brown the crumble.

8. Remove the tray from the oven and allow the crumble to cool completely.

9. To make the vanilla chantilly, in a medium bowl, combine the cream and sugar (you can add more sugar if you prefer).

Hand blender

Stand mixer, with the
paddle attachment

Baking tray/sheet

10. Use a knife to cut the vanilla bean lengthwise and scrape the beans from the center. Add the beans to the cream mixture. Whisk until the mixture forms medium peaks, being careful not to over whip it.

11. To assemble the sundae pots, remove the ice cream from the freezer and let it soften for 5 minutes.

12. To a small glass jar, add a few tablespoons of cocoa crumble. Dip an ice cream scoop into hot water, then dry it off. Scoop a large heaping of ice cream and place it atop the crumble.

13. Spoon the chantilly atop the ice cream (or use a piping bag to be fancy!). Drizzle the salted caramel over the chantilly before serving. Repeat this process for the remaining sundaes. This will make 6–8 pots depending on the size of your pots.

CHAPTER 6

dough

Everyday Sandwich Loaf

MAKES 1 LOAF

FOR THE PRE-FERMENT

200g water

1g instant dry yeast

200g all-purpose/plain flour

FOR THE DOUGH

285g bread/white bread flour,
   plus more for dusting

100g water

12g unsalted butter, cubed

10g sea salt

0.5g instant dry yeast

4g granulated/caster sugar

Neutral/vegetable oil,
   for coating

SPECIAL EQUIPMENT

Stand mixer, with the dough
   hook attachment

2lb (900g) loaf pan/tin

Baking tray/sheet

Razor blade

Instant read thermometer

Learning to use pre-ferments is an easy way to improve the flavor and texture of your dough with very little effort. Here, we are using a poolish, which is a fairly wet pre-ferment that we leave overnight. This addition of poolish requires very little additional yeast and gives the loaf a soft interior.

1. To make the pre-ferment, in a medium bowl, combine the water and yeast. Stir with a spatula until the yeast has dissolved, then add the flour. Mix until fully combined. Cover the bowl with plastic wrap/cling film and leave it at room temperature for 12 hours. Once it's ready, the pre-ferment should have lots of little bubbles on the surface.

2. In the bowl of a stand mixer fitted with the dough hook, combine the pre-ferment and all the dough ingredients. Knead the dough on medium-low speed for 5 minutes. Stop the mixer, allow the dough to rest for 5 minutes, then knead again for 5 minutes. The dough should now be smooth.

3. Transfer the dough to a lightly oiled bowl, keeping it in a rough ball shape. Cover the bowl with plastic wrap and allow the dough to rise for 2 hours, or until doubled in size.

4. Punch the dough to knock the air out of it and then carefully transfer the dough, smooth-side down, to a lightly floured work surface. Use your fingers to press the dough into a rough rectangle shape.

5. Starting from the top of the rectangle, fold the dough in on itself, almost like you're rolling the dough into a sausage. Pinch the seam together.

6. Carefully transfer the dough seam-side down to a lightly oiled 2-pound (900g) loaf pan. Lightly cover the pan with plastic wrap/clingfilm and allow the dough to rise for about 2 hours. The dough should roughly double in size and should be close to level with the top of the pan, so keep a close eye on it.

7. Preheat the oven to 445°F/230°C. Place a tray at the bottom of the oven.

8. Use a sieve to lightly dust the top of the loaf with bread flour, and then, using a razor blade, confidently slash the loaf vertically down the center.

9. Place the bread in the center of the oven and splash a small cup of water on the hot tray (this creates steam). Bake for 15 minutes.

10. Lower the temperature to 375°F/190°C and bake for 25–30 minutes. The bread should look nice and golden on top. It should read an internal temperature of around 194–203°F/90–95°C with a digital thermometer.

11. Remove the bread from the oven and tip it from the pan onto a rack. Allow it to cool completely so the crumb can fully set before serving.

Sea Salt Focaccia

MAKES 1 LOAF

FOR THE PRE-FERMENT

170g bread/white bread flour

170g water

2.5g instant dry yeast

FOR THE DOUGH

350g water

5.5g instant dry yeast

515g bread/white bread flour

30g olive oil, plus more for greasing and dimpling

12g flaky sea salt, plus extra for topping

SPECIAL EQUIPMENT

13 × 9 × 2-inch (33 × 23 × 5cm) baking pan/tin

By taking the pre-ferment technique from Tier 1 (page 164), we can get the same flavor and texture qualities into our focaccia, but make it a little more challenging, using a much wetter dough. The high hydration means the dough is much looser, so slightly harder to handle, but it will leave us with a lovely open crumb, that is soft and the perfect loaf to share. Get as creative as you want with the toppings too!

1. To make the pre-ferment, in a medium bowl, combine the flour, water, and yeast. Mix well with a spatula. Cover the bowl with plastic wrap/cling film and set aside for 12 hours. Once it's ready, the pre-ferment should have lots of little bubbles on the surface.

2. To make the dough, in a large bowl, combine the water and yeast. Swirl the mixture together to dissolve the yeast into the water.

3. Add the flour, olive oil, salt, and the pre-ferment. Use your hands or a spatula to mix the ingredients together until they form a shaggy dough and there are no more dry bits. You're not kneading the dough—just mixing the ingredients together.

4. Cover the bowl with a slightly damp kitchen/tea towel and allow the dough to rest for 30 minutes.

5. You're going to perform the first "stretch and fold" procedure. This is essentially another technique to knead the dough and build strength by developing the gluten. Lightly wet one hand and place it on the underside of the dough in the bowl. Grab the dough and stretch it out and up. Fold this piece of dough into the center, then turn the bowl 90° and repeat this process. You're going to do this 4 times total. The dough might initially be slightly tough while it's still shaggy, but as you progress, the dough will become much more elastic. Cover the bowl and set it aside for 30 minutes.

6. After the dough has rested, perform another 4 stretch and folds. You'll notice the dough becoming much more voluminous and elastic. Try to handle it relatively gently so you don't remove too much air. Cover the dough and set aside for 30 minutes.

7. Repeat this process twice more at 30-minute intervals. In total you will perform 16 stretch and folds over 2 hours

8. After the final stretch and fold, transfer the dough to an oiled 13 × 9 × 2-inch (33 × 23 × 5cm) baking pan. Use your fingers to press the dough as best as possible into the edges of the pan. Don't worry if the dough retracts or doesn't reach the edge because, as it proofs and relaxes, it will spread out.

9. Cover the pan with lightly oiled plastic wrap and proof for 1 hour at room temperature.

10. Preheat the oven to 445°F/230°C.

11. The dough should have spread to the edges and started to rise up the pan. Drizzle more olive oil on top of the dough and use your fingertips to dimple the entire dough, gently pressing to the bottom of the pan. Sprinkle flaky sea salt over the top. You can also get creative and add any toppings you fancy, such as rosemary, tomatoes, red onions, etc.

12. Place the pan in the oven and bake for 25–30 minutes, or until the focaccia is a deep golden brown color.

13. Remove the pan from the oven. Transfer the focaccia from the pan to a rack. You can place the focaccia and rack in the oven for 5 minutes to add a little extra crunch to the bottom and edges. Otherwise, you can serve the bread now or allow it to cool for serving later.

Raspberry Jam Donuts

MAKES 14 DONUTS

FOR THE DONUT DOUGH

500g all-purpose/plain flour,
plus more for flouring

50g granulated/caster sugar

10g sea salt

7g instant dry yeast

50g unsalted butter,
room temperature

275g whole milk,
room temperature

2g lemon zest

1 tsp vanilla bean paste

120g eggs, room temperature

Neutral/vegetable oil,
for coating

Nonstick cooking spray

70–100oz (about 2–3 liters)
vegetable oil, for frying

200g granulated/caster sugar,
for coating

Raspberry jam, for filling

There's something so enticing about a big tray full of sugary jam donuts behind a bakery window. The eggs and butter in the dough make this almost brioche-like, resulting in a soft, pillowy, fragrant donut. It's a slightly long process, but chilling the dough makes it much easier to work with and improves the flavor.

1. In the bowl of a stand mixer fitted with the dough hook, combine the flour, sugar, salt, yeast, and butter. Start mixing on low speed.

2. In a tall measuring cup/jug, whisk together the milk, lemon, vanilla, and eggs.

3. With the mixer on medium-low speed, slowly add the wet ingredients. Keep mixing just until there are no more dry ingredients and everything has been fully incorporated. You may need to pause to scrape down the bowl a few times to ensure all the dry bits on the bottom get fully incorporated.

4. Remove the bowl from the mixer and cover with a damp kitchen towel. Allow the dough to rest for 30 minutes.

5. Return the bowl to the mixer and knead on medium for 12–15 minutes. Very lightly flour your fingertips and grab a small piece of dough. Stretch this out gently, and if the dough forms a "windowpane," this means the dough is ready and enough gluten has been developed (page 38). The dough should appear smooth and elastic.

6. Use a bench scraper to transfer the dough to a very lightly floured work surface. Lightly flour your hands and shape the dough into a ball. Carefully transfer the dough to a lightly oiled large bowl.

7. Spray the top of the dough with nonstick cooking spray and then cover the bowl with plastic wrap/cling film. Refrigerate the dough for a minimum of 6 hours or overnight. Because the dough is enriched, it will be much easier to work with after refrigeration.

8. Spray two large baking trays with nonstick cooking spray. Cut 14 pieces of parchment paper into squares measuring 3 × 3 inches (8 × 8cm). Place these on the trays and spray them with nonstick cooking spray.

9. Place the dough on your work surface. Use a bench scraper to cut the dough into 65g pieces, then shape these into tight balls. To do this, very lightly flour your hands, but don't add much—if any at all—to the work surface. Shape your hand into a "C" and form a cup around the dough ball. Quickly rotate the dough underneath your hand to form a tight ball.

Stand mixer, with the dough hook attachment

Bench scraper

2× large baking trays

Instant read thermometer

Piping bag, plus a small round tip nozzle

Chopstick or wooden dowel

10. Place the balls on the parchment squares and spray the tops of the balls with nonstick cooking spray. Gently press the balls down to flatten them into a disk shape.

11. Cover the balls with plastic wrap/cling film and allow them to proof at room temperature. The proofing time is crucial because this is the key to getting that perfect white ring around the middle of the donuts. You're looking for the balls to almost triple in size (about 3 inches [8cm] wide by the time they're proofed). Depending on the room's temperature, this can take anywhere from 1 to 3 hours—or longer if it's cold—so keep an eye on them.

12. Heat the oil to 340°F/170°C in a deep fryer (or in a large pot). I like to fry a test donut to see if the dough has properly proofed. Carefully place a dough ball in the fryer and gently peel off the parchment paper. Fry the donut for 90 seconds, flip, fry for 90 seconds, flip, fry for 30 seconds, flip, and fry for 30 seconds, for a total of 4 minutes.

13. Transfer the donut to a rack. If the dough has properly proofed, you should see a nice white band along the center of the donut. When you cut into the donut, it will have a fluffy center. If the donut has no ring and feels dense, continue proofing the remaining dough balls.

14. If you're happy with the proofing, continue frying the remaining dough balls. Depending on the size of your fryer, it is best to do these in batches of 1–3, to avoid the temperature of the oil dropping.

15. Place the sugar in a small bowl or on a wide plate. Toss them in the sugar to gently coat them.

16. Fill a piping bag fitted with a small round tip nozzle with the raspberry jam. Pierce a hole in the side of each donut using a chopstick or wooden dowel and fill with jam until it feels heavy. Serve immediately.

Boston Cream Pie Donuts

MAKES 14 DONUTS

1 batch Donut Dough
  (page 168)

**FOR THE BROWN SUGAR
CRÈME PÂTISSIERÈ**

2 fresh vanilla pods

720g whole milk

215g egg yolks

110g light brown sugar

Pinch sea salt

65g cornstarch/corn flour

70g unsalted butter, cold
  and cubed

**FOR THE DARK
CHOCOLATE GLAZE**

300g dark chocolate, 70%
  cocoa solids

30g water

35g honey

90g unsalted butter

SPECIAL EQUIPMENT

Chopstick or wooden dowel

Piping bag, plus a small
  round tip nozzle

Summers as a kid were spent in America with my mum's family, just outside of Boston. Donuts were a breakfast staple, and there would always be a Boston cream pie in the box. We're taking the same Tier 1 donut recipe (page 168) and making the classic Boston cream pie a little fancier.

1. Prepare the donut dough as per page 168. While the dough is chilling overnight, start the Brown Sugar Crème Pâtissierè.

2. Take the vanilla beans and cut them lengthwise. Scrape the seeds out of the center with a knife, and add these to a medium saucepan along with the milk. Place it over medium heat, until it is steaming, but not boiling.

3. While that heats up, add the egg yolks, sugar, salt, and cornstarch to a medium bowl. Whisk this for one minute until thick.

4. Once the milk is hot, slowly pour this over the egg yolk mixture, whisking constantly. Pour it all back into the pan, keep it over medium heat, and whisk continuously until it begins to thicken. Once the mixture starts to bubble, cook for a further minute, then remove it from the heat and immediately pass it through a fine-mesh sieve on top of a clean bowl.

5. Press the mixture through with a spatula, then add in the butter and whisk until there are no more lumps.

6. Place plastic wrap/cling film directly on the surface and refrigerate overnight (or a minimum of 4 hours).

7. Once the donut dough is ready, shape, proof ,and fry them according to page 168.

8. When the donuts have cooled slightly, remove the crème pâtissierè from the fridge and whisk to loosen it, so that it is nice and smooth. Add this into a piping bag, fitted with a round tip nozzle.

9. Pierce the side of a donut with a chopstick, and then place the piping nozzle inside. Squeeze the piping bag, filling the donut with the crème pâtissierè until it feels heavy. Repeat this with the remaining donuts.

10. For the chocolate glaze, add all of the ingredients into a medium bowl. Place it over a pan of gently simmering water, and stir together until completely melted.

11. Once melted, let it cool for a minute, until it is roughly 86°F/30°C and then take the donuts and dunk the top into the chocolate glaze.

12. Let any excess drip off, then quickly flip them over and place them onto a wire rack to set, before serving.

Brioche

MAKES 2 LOAVES

320g eggs, plus more for
  egg wash

25g whole milk

490g all-purpose/plain flour,
  plus more for dusting

50g granulated/caster sugar

12g sea salt

9g fresh yeast or 4.5g instant
  dry yeast

270g unsalted butter, slightly
  softened, cut into pieces,
  plus more for greasing

Neutral/vegetable oil,
  for coating

There's nothing that quite compares to the buttery, yeasty smell you get from a loaf of brioche straight out of the oven. Brioche is an enriched dough, which can be more difficult to handle due to the higher levels of fat compared to a traditional loaf of bread. By starting with this brioche, we can learn how to work with enriched doughs, which opens up a whole world of baked goods to create.

1. Add the eggs, milk, flour, sugar, salt, and yeast into the bowl of a stand mixer fitted with the dough hook.

2. Knead the dough on medium-low speed for 10 minutes. During the mixing, you may need to pause to scrape down the side of the bowl.

3. After 10 minutes, add the butter a little at a time. Allow each piece to be incorporated into the dough before adding the next.

4. Once you've added all the butter, increase the speed to medium and knead for 10–15 minutes, regularly pausing to scrape the sides of the bowl. The dough is ready when it cleanly pulls away from the sides of the bowl and you can stretch it out with your fingers into a thin transparent dough. This is the "windowpane" test (see page 38). The time it takes to knead will depend on the power of your mixer, so you might have to knead a little longer.

5. Transfer the dough to a lightly floured surface. Use a bench scraper to round the dough into a tight boule (ball), then transfer the dough to a bowl which has been lightly coated with oil. Cover the bowl with plastic wrap/cling film and allow to proof at room temperature for 1 hour, or until doubled in size.

6. Remove the dough from the bowl and use your hands to gently knock the air out. Shape it into a tight boule again and return it to the lightly oiled bowl. Press a sheet of plastic wrap/cling film directly onto the surface of the dough (this will prevent it from forming a skin) and then wrap another piece tightly over the top of the bowl. Refrigerate the dough overnight.

7. Remove the dough from the bowl and cut it into 80g pieces.

8. Lightly flour your hands and cup your hand over the dough, creating a "C" shape, and tuck the dough under the palm of your hand. Moving your hand quickly in a circular motion, roll the dough to create tension and form the dough into a tighter ball. Repeat this with the remaining dough balls.

9. Lift the balls, evenly spaced, into 2 lightly buttered 2-pound (900g) loaf pans. You should be able to get about 6 dough balls in each pan.

Stand mixer, with the dough
  hook attachment

Bench scraper

2× 2lb (900g) loaf pans

Instant read thermometer

10. Cover the pans with plastic wrap and allow the dough to rise for 3–4 hours at room temperature. The balls should double in size, look puffy and be touching each other. The time it takes will depend on your room temperature, so keep an eye on them.

11. Preheat the oven to 355°F/180°C. Give the dough a light egg wash once proofed.

12. Place the pans in the oven and bake for around 35 minutes, or until a deep golden brown. If you want to be precise, the internal temperature of the dough should be around 203°F/95°C when fully baked.

13. Let the breads cool for a few minutes before tipping it out onto a rack and allow the brioche to cool before serving.

TWO
TIER

Soft Brioche Cinnamon Rolls

MAKES 9 CINNAMON ROLLS

FOR THE DOUGH

120g whole milk

270g eggs

600g all-purpose/plain flour, plus more for flouring

7.5g instant dry yeast

50g granulated/caster sugar

7g sea salt

230g unsalted butter, softened, cut into pieces, plus more for greasing

Neutral/vegetable oil, for coating

FOR THE FILLING

300g light brown sugar

15g ground cinnamon

200g unsalted butter, softened

FOR THE FROSTING

90g unsalted butter, softened

200g full-fat cream cheese

½ tsp vanilla bean paste

120g powdered/icing sugar

¼ tsp sea salt

By mastering the Tier 1 brioche (page 174), you'll have a great understanding of handling enriched doughs. We'll apply this same knowledge to creating an enriched brioche for our cinnamon rolls, that we fill with a cinnamon-sugar butter and top with a luscious cream cheese frosting. If you've ever wondered how to get the perfect spiral then the technique for cutting the dough into strips and rolling them up is a game changer! These are best fresh out of the oven but stay nice and soft if you need to eat them later, just heat them up slightly, and serve.

1. In the bowl of a stand mixer fitted with the dough hook attachment, combine the milk, eggs, flour, dry yeast, sugar, and salt. Knead on medium-low for 7 minutes, pausing to scrape down the sides as needed.

2. Add the butter a piece at a time. Allow each piece to be fully incorporated into the dough before adding the next.

3. Increase the speed to medium and knead the dough for 10–12 minutes, pausing to scrape the sides of the bowl if anything is stuck. To check that the dough is done, lightly flour your fingers and grab a small piece of dough. Gently stretch it, and if it forms a thin transparent window without tearing—also known as the "windowpane test"—the dough is ready (see page 38).

4. Transfer the dough to a lightly floured surface—it will be quite sticky but be confident with it—and lightly flour the top of the dough. Use a bench scraper to round the dough into a tight boule (ball), then transfer to a lightly oiled bowl. Cover the bowl with plastic wrap/cling film and allow to proof at room temperature for 1 hour, or until doubled in size.

5. Remove the dough from the bowl and use your hands to gently knock the air out of the dough. Lightly flour again and shape the dough into a tight boule. Place the ball back in the lightly oiled bowl. Lightly oil your hands and rub a thin layer on the top of the dough to prevent it from forming a tough skin. Cover the bowl tightly with plastic wrap/cling film and refrigerate overnight. This will make the dough much easier to work with and also develop more flavor.

6. In the bowl of a stand mixer fitted with the paddle attachment, combine the brown sugar, cinnamon, and soft butter. Beat on medium for 2–3 minutes, or until smooth, light, and fluffy. It's important that this mixture is quite soft because if it's too cold, it could tear the dough as you try to spread it. Set this mixture aside.

SPECIAL EQUIPMENT

Stand mixer, with the dough
  hook attachment

Bench scraper

9 × 9-inch (23 × 23cm) baking
  pan/tin

Rolling pin

7. Grease a 9 × 9-inch (23 × 23cm) pan with softened butter and line the base and sides with parchment paper. Parchment paper on the bottom will prevent the cinnamon butter from caramelizing too much as the rolls bake.

8. Transfer the chilled dough to a lightly floured surface and press the dough into a rough square with your hands. Use a lightly floured rolling pin to roll the dough into a rectangle, about 21 × 14-inches (53 × 36cm). As you're rolling, flour the top and the underside of the dough as needed to prevent it from sticking.

9. Use a sharp knife or a cutting wheel to trim the rectangle to about 19 × 12-inches (48 × 30.5cm).

10. Evenly spread the cinnamon butter across the entire dough, leaving about a ½-inch (1.3cm) gap at the top edge farthest from you. Spread a small amount of softened butter along this uncovered edge. This will help seal the dough.

11. With the long edge of the dough facing you, cut the dough vertically into 9 strips, each about 1½ inches (4cm) wide. The easiest way to do this is with a multi-wheel pastry cutter, but a regular pizza wheel will also work!

12. Starting from the bottom edge closest to you, roll 1 strip into a tight spiral. Flip it onto its side and you should have a perfectly spiraled cinnamon roll. Place this in the prepared pan and repeat the rolling with the remaining strips. As you place the rolls into the pan, ensure you leave enough room in between each one so they can properly proof.

13. Cover the pan with plastic wrap and allow the rolls to proof at room temperature for 1 hour, or until doubled in size. They should look nice and puffy when they are ready and should just be touching. While they proof, preheat the oven to 355°F/180°C.

14. Place the pan in the oven and bake the rolls for about 30 minutes or until they have a golden brown color. Remove the pan from the oven and place it on a rack.

15. In the bowl of a stand mixer fitted with the paddle attachment, combine the butter, cream cheese, and vanilla. Sift the powdered sugar and salt over the top, then beat for 1–2 minutes on medium or until the frosting is completely smooth.

16. Once the rolls have cooled for about 20–30 minutes, spread the cream cheese frosting over the top before serving. These are always best served slightly warm, but they'll stay soft if you need to eat them later on.

Tangzhong Garlic Dough Balls

**MAKES 16–18
DOUGH BALLS**

FOR THE TANGZHONG

105g whole milk

21g bread/white bread flour

FOR THE DOUGH

440g bread/white bread flour

205g water

8g instant dry yeast

6g granulated/caster sugar

7g sea salt

45g olive oil, plus more
 for coating

FOR THE GARLIC BUTTER

75g unsalted butter, softened

2 garlic cloves, finely grated

Pinch of sea salt

Pinch of freshly ground
 black pepper

1 tsp olive oil

30g panko breadcrumbs

Small parmesan wedge, for
 topping

Chopped chives, for topping

Sesame seeds, for topping

My cooking skills don't quite match up to my baking skills, but any time I'm cooking something vaguely Italian, I'm serving it with these garlic dough balls. To create perfectly soft dough, we are using a popular technique known as the tangzhong method. Cooking a small portion of the flour and liquid creates a thick paste that allows the starches to pre-gelatinize, which when added to the dough, creates a soft, tender loaf. The secret element is the crunchy panko base, which adds a little hidden texture and soaks up all that garlic butter.

1. To make the tangzhong, add the milk and flour to a medium saucepan over low heat. Whisk until the mixture begins to form a thick paste. Remove the saucepan from the heat. Transfer the mixture to a medium bowl and allow it to cool for 10 minutes.

2. In the bowl of a stand mixer fitted with the dough hook, combine all the dough ingredients and add the tangzhong mixture on top. Knead on medium-low speed for 4–5 minutes, or until the dough is smooth and comes away cleanly from the sides of the bowl. (You might need to pause to scrape down the sides a few times in case anything gets stuck!)

3. Carefully transfer the dough to a very lightly floured work surface and use your hands to shape it into a smooth round ball. Place the ball in a lightly oiled bowl and cover the bowl with plastic wrap/cling film. Allow the dough to rise at room temperature for 1 hour or until doubled in size.

4. In a small bowl, make the garlic butter by combining all the ingredients. Stir until completely smooth. Spread about ⅓ of the garlic butter on the inside of a 10-inch (25cm) round baking pan. Add the breadcrumbs and shake the pan to cover all the inner surfaces with the breadcrumbs. Tip out any excess.

5. Once proofed, remove the dough from the bowl and gently press the dough on your work surface to remove the air. Use a dough scraper to cut the dough into 45g pieces—you should get around 16–18 dough balls.

6. Gently flatten each piece with your hand into a rough circle. For each circle, lift edges and fold toward the center, which should result in a tight ball. Flip each ball over so the seam is now facing down. Cup your hand over the dough, creating a C shape, and tuck the dough under the palm of your hand. Moving your hand quickly in a circular motion, roll the dough to create tension and form the dough into a tighter ball.

SPECIAL EQUIPMENT

Stand mixer, with the dough
  hook attachment

10-inch (25cm) round baking
  pan/tin

7. Place the dough balls in the pan, leaving about 1 inch (2.5cm) between each ball. Lightly cover the pan with very lightly oiled plastic wrap. Allow the dough to proof for 1 hour. The balls should double in size and touch each other.

8. Preheat the oven to 345°F/175°C.

9. Place the pan in the oven and bake the balls for 40–45 minutes or until they have a deep golden brown color.

10. Remove the pan from the oven and slather more garlic butter over the top, saving some for dipping.

11. Shave fresh parmesan over the top along with chopped chives and sesame seeds and serve the dough balls immediately.

Chia and Black Sesame Shokupan

MAKES 1 LOAF

FOR THE YUDANE

62g bread/white bread flour

56g boiling water

FOR THE DOUGH

225g bread/white bread flour,
plus more for flouring

25g whole wheat/wholemeal
bread

5.5g instant dry yeast

5g sea salt

10g mixed seeds (chia and
black sesame)

7g honey

170g whole milk

15g unsalted butter, softened,
plus more for greasing and
topping

Neutral/vegetable oil,
for coating

Taking inspiration from the tangzhong method in the Tier 1 dough balls (page 180), we are going to use a similar pre-gelatinized mixture in the dough—a yudane. This is a slightly thicker, more gelatinous paste that involves pouring boiling water over the flour. This creates an especially soft dough, which is iconic with the Japanese shokupan. The difficulty lies in the shaping of the loaf, which is different to a classic loaf recipe, requiring you to flatten the dough with a rolling pin and then roll it tightly on itself to create the two barrels of dough. The shokupan is perfect to eat with butter or served as sandwich bread.

1. To make the yudane, in a medium bowl, combine the flour and boiling water. Stir with a spatula until it forms a thick sticky dough. Cover the bowl with plastic wrap/cling film and refrigerate for 4 hours.

2. To make the dough, in the bowl of a stand mixer fitted with the dough hook, combine all the dough ingredients except the butter and add the yudane. Knead on medium-low for 2–3 minutes, or until everything has pulled together and there are no more dry bits. If there are any remaining dry bits, add just a touch more milk.

3. Add the butter and knead on medium speed for about 12–14 minutes. Because of the yudane, it takes a little longer for this dough to develop, but once it's ready, it should pass the windowpane test: Grab a small piece of dough and gently stretch this between your fingers. If the dough forms a windowpane without tearing easily, you've developed enough gluten (see page 38).

4. Transfer the dough to a lightly floured work surface. Shape the dough into a smooth ball and place it into a lightly oiled bowl. Cover with plastic wrap/ cling film and allow the dough to rise for 45 minutes–1 hour. It should double in size.

5. Transfer the dough to a lightly floured surface. Punch the dough to knock the air out. Weigh the dough and cut it into two equal pieces, roughly 270g per piece.

6. Use your hand to gently flatten one piece of dough and use a floured rolling pin to roll it into a long rectangle shape that's roughly the same width as your bread pan.

7. Flip the rectangle over, and starting from the short edge of the rectangle, roll it up on itself into a log shape with a nice tight spiral. Repeat this process with the second piece of dough.

8. Place the spirals seam-side down and side-by-side into a very lightly greased 1-pound (450g) loaf pan.

9. Cover the pan with plastic wrap and proof for a further 45 minutes–1 hour. The dough should double in size. If you poke the dough, it should slowly bounce back.

10. Preheat the oven to 375°F/190°C.

11. Place the pan in the oven and bake the dough for about 35 minutes, or until a deep golden color forms on the top. Once the bread has baked, I like to remove it from the pan and return it to the oven, directly on the wire rack, for 5 minutes more to crisp up the outside edges just slightly.

12. Transfer the pan to a rack and quickly brush the top with butter. Allow it to cool completely before serving.

Multi-Seed Bloomer

MAKES 1 LOAF

275g bread/white bread flour

225g whole wheat/wholemeal
  bread flour

12g sea salt

5g instant dry yeast

370g room temperature water

1 tsp honey (8g)

105g mixed seeds, divided
  (an equal mix of sunflower,
  pumpkin, sesame
  and poppy)

Neutral/vegetable oil,
  for coating

SPECIAL EQUIPMENT

2× baking trays/sheets

Small baking tray/sheet

Razor blade

Instant read thermometer

A hearty multi-seed loaf is always great to have in your repertoire. I developed this recipe to be made by hand, but feel free to use a stand mixer if you prefer. Using whole wheat/wholemeal flour makes the dough slightly more absorbent, so it is easier to handle as a beginner baker

1. In a large bowl, combine the flours, salt, and yeast.

2. Add the water and honey. Use your hand to mix the ingredients together until they form a shaggy dough and all the flour has been incorporated.

3. Transfer the dough to a very lightly floured work surface and knead with your hands for 7–10 minutes, or until the dough feels smooth and elastic (see page 38).

4. Add 70g of the mixed seeds and knead the dough until they're evenly distributed. Shape the dough into a rough ball and place it in a lightly oiled bowl. Cover the bowl with plastic wrap/cling film and proof at room temperature for 1½ hours.

5. Spread out the remaining mixed seeds on a baking tray and set aside.

6. The dough should have doubled in size. Place the dough smooth-side down on your lightly floured work surface. Use your fingertips to press the dough into a rough circle shape.

7. Working your way around the dough, use your hand to stitch the dough, folding the edges so that they meet in the middle and are joined together. Flip it over and gently cup your hands around the underside of the dough, rotating it on the work surface to create some tension.

8. Carefully flip the boule (ball), smooth-side down, onto the tray with the remaining mixed seeds. Rock the dough in a circular motion to cover it in seeds. Flip the dough back over, onto a baking tray lined with a sheet of parchment. Loosely cover the dough with plastic wrap and allow to rise for 1½ hours.

9. Preheat the oven to 390°F/200°C. Place a small baking tray on the bottom of the oven.

10. Use a razor blade to quickly slash 3 lines, evenly spaced, on the top of the dough. Quickly place the tray in the oven and splash a small cup of water to the tray at the bottom of the oven. Bake for 40–45 minutes.

11. Once baked, it should reach an internal temperature of around 195–203°F /90–95°C with an instant read thermometer. Remove the tray from the oven and allow the bread to cool completely on a wire rack before slicing.

Oat and Flaxseed Loaf

MAKES 1 LOAF

35g jumbo rolled oats

35g golden flaxseed/linseed

70g boiling water

340g bread/white bread flour,
    plus more for dusting

30g whole wheat/wholemeal
    bread flour

195g water

7g sea salt

5.5g instant dry yeast

10g honey

Neutral/vegetable oil,
    for coating

SPECIAL EQUIPMENT

Stand mixer, with the dough
    hook attachment

2lb (900g) loaf pan/tin

Instant read thermometer

Small baking tray/sheet

Razor blade

In this loaf, we are using "soakers"—oats and flaxseed. If we throw these into a recipe dry, they'll soak up the moisture in the recipe and result in a dry loaf of bread. Therefore, it is important to hydrate these ingredients by pre-soaking them in water.

1. In a medium bowl, combine the rolled oats and flaxseed. Add boiling water over the top and stir until soggy. Set aside for 15 minutes.

2. In the bowl of a stand mixer fitted with the dough hook, combine the oat mixture, the flours, water, salt, yeast, and honey. Knead on medium speed for about 8 minutes until the dough is smooth.

3. Transfer the dough to a lightly floured work surface. Shape the dough into a rough boule (ball) and transfer it to a lightly oiled bowl. Cover with plastic wrap/cling film and proof for 1 hour at room temperature.

4. Transfer the dough to a lightly floured surface. Flip the dough so the smooth side faces down, then use your fingertips to press the dough into a rough "A" shape (slightly narrower at the top and widening at the base).

5. Starting from the top of the "A," roll the dough onto itself, pressing and sealing the dough with your thumbs as you roll it into a tight log shape. Pinch the seam of the dough together.

6. Roll the dough over and place it seam-side down into a lightly greased 2-pound (900g) loaf pan. Cover with plastic wrap/cling film and proof for 1 hour more at room temperature. The dough should double in size in the pan.

7. Preheat the oven to 445°F/230°C. Place a tray in the bottom of the oven.

8. Use a small sieve to dust a light coating of bread flour over the top of the dough. Use a sharp razor blade to quickly and confidently slash lines horizontally across the dough.

9. Place the pan in the center of the oven and quickly splash a small cup of water on tray at the bottom of the oven. (Bake for 15 minutes.)

10. Lower the temperature to 375°F/190°C and bake for 20 minutes more.

11. Remove the pan from the oven and carefully remove the bread from the pan. Place the loaf directly on the oven rack and bake for 5 minutes more. The internal temperature of the dough should read around 194–203°F / 90–95°C if you insert an instant read thermometer in the middle.

12. Remove the loaf from the oven and transfer it to a wire rack. Allow it to cool completely so the crumb fully sets.

Hazelnut Praline Mille-Feuille

MAKES 1 LARGE MILLE-FEUILLE

½ batch Diplomat Cream
(page 211)

½ batch Hazelnut Praline
Paste (page 227)

FOR THE PUFF PASTRY

295g all-purpose/plain flour,
plus more for dusting

7g sea salt

45g unsalted butter, melted

147g tepid water

3g white vinegar

FOR THE BUTTER BLOCK

250g unsalted butter, slightly
softened, plus more

Powdered/icing sugar
for dusting

A mille-feuille is the perfect recipe for learning the fundamentals of laminated doughs. Here you can begin to understand incorporating butter into a dough and rolling it by hand to create lots of flakey layers. The beauty of this is that although it requires a few more steps compared to other laminated doughs, puff pastry is not yeasted, so you have slightly more time to work with the dough and hone your laminating. We fill it with a smooth diplomat cream and a sweet hazelnut praline, which adds a hint of nutty, caramelized flavors.

1. Make the crème pâtissierè for the Diplomat Cream, then cover and chill in the fridge until you are ready to assemble.

2. Prepare the Hazelnut Praline Paste. Leave it covered at room temperature so that it can cool down before you are ready to pipe.

3. To make the pastry, in the bowl of a stand mixer fitted with the paddle attachment, combine the flour and salt.

4. In a tall measuring jug/cup, combine the butter, water, and vinegar. Stir well to combine (the vinegar helps relax the gluten in the pastry).

5. With the mixer running on medium-low, slowly pour in the butter mixture. Continue to mix just until the dough starts to pull together and there are no more dry bits in the bowl. The dough will look shaggy.

6. Transfer the dough to a work surface and use your hands to briefly knead until it's slightly smoother. Shape it into a rough rectangle shape, then wrap in plastic wrap/cling film. Refrigerate for 2 hours.

7. Place the slightly softened butter in the center of one half of a large sheet of parchment paper (about 20 inches [51cm] long). Fold the other half over the top, then fold the sides and the edges of the paper underneath to form a 7 × 8-inch (18 × 20cm) block. Flip the block over so the folded edges are underneath.

8. Use a rolling pin to roll the butter across the block of parchment paper, ensuring you reach the corners. You should end up with a neat, even block of butter. Refrigerate until firm. Before you start to roll out the puff pastry dough, you need to get your butter to a point where it's cold but flexible to ensure proper lamination of the dough. The butter needs to be around 55–57°F/13°–14°C before you can add it to your dough. Any colder and it will crack. If it's too warm, it will leak as you roll.

9. Just before the butter is at temperature, lightly flour the work surface and remove the puff pastry from the fridge. Roll the dough into a rough rectangle,

Stand mixer, with the
  paddle attachment

Rolling pin

Pastry wheel

Instant read thermometer

4× baking trays/sheets

2× perforated silicone
  baking mats

2× piping bags, plus 1 large
  round tip nozzle

about 7½ inches (19cm) wide and 18 inches (46cm) long.

10. Unwrap the butter and place it in the center of the rectangle. Fold the left third of dough into the center of the butter block and then the right third of dough into the center of the butter block, creating a seam where the dough meets.

11. Use your fingers to seal the seam together and then seal the edges of dough around the sides so the butter is completely encased and none of it is visible.

12. Work quickly here or the butter and dough will become too warm. Lightly flour the pastry block, and with the seam horizontally in front of you, roll the dough just a few times to give it some slight width. Then rotate the dough 90° so the seam is now in line with you vertically and begin to roll the dough into a long rectangular shape. Don't worry too much about the length of the rectangle but more about the thickness of it. You want it to be about 0.2–0.4 inches (0.5–1cm) thick (or thereabouts). Try to ensure as you're rolling that you're keeping the rectangle shape as neat as possible.

13. Dust off any excess flour and then use a pastry wheel just to trim off any small wonky edges so you have a neat rectangle. Then perform your first single fold (also known as a "letter fold"). Take the top third of the dough and fold it slightly over halfway. Then take the bottom third of the dough and fold this over the top—just like you're folding a letter.

14. At this point, you need to roll the dough out again, just as you did in step 12. Roll the dough to give it some width, rotate it 90°, and then roll it out into a long rectangle. This second roll depends on the temperature of your dough. If you feel the dough is extremely soft, then wrap it in plastic wrap/cling film and refrigerate for 10–15 minutes. Always work with the dough when it's cool but flexible. You want it to be at a temperature where the butter is cold but pliable—just like before.

15. Once you've rolled the dough into a rectangle for the second time, perform a single fold again. Wrap the dough in plastic wrap/cling film and refrigerate for 30 minutes.

16. Remove the dough from the fridge. Repeat the whole process again for the third and fourth folds, then refrigerate the dough for 30 minutes. Make sure to monitor the dough's temperature. If you feel it's too soft after the third fold, refrigerate the dough before performing the fourth fold.

17. Meanwhile, finish the Diplomat Cream by adding the whipped cream, and then refrigerating for 2 hours.

18. Remove the dough from the fridge. Repeat the process again for fifth and sixth folds, then refrigerate the dough for 30 more minutes. Preheat the oven to 430°F/220°C.

19. Place the dough on a lightly floured surface and roll it into a rough rectangle just slightly smaller than your baking tray and about 0.23-inch/6mm thick.

20. Lift the dough onto a baking tray lined with a perforated baking mat (or parchment paper). Place a second baking mat on top along with another baking tray. Now you need to weigh the tray down so that pastry only puffs up slightly as it bakes. Add around 1.7kg of weight, evenly distributed across the top baking tray. I use two heavy baking trays.

21. Place the tray into the oven and bake for 10 minutes, then immediately lower the temperature to 375°F/190°C and bake for a further 40–45 minutes.

22. Remove the tray from the oven, and lift off the weight along with the top baking tray and mat. The pastry should be an even, light golden color all over.

23. Place it back in the oven, uncovered, for a further 5 minutes or until it is a deeper golden color.

24. Remove it from the oven, and increase the temperature to 390°F/200°C. Dust the top with an even layer of powdered/icing sugar then place it back in the oven.

25. Keep a very close eye on it, and cook for 5 minutes or until the sugar has disappeared, and the pastry has a caramelized, glassy finish. It can burn very quickly so be careful. Remove from the oven to cool for 30 minutes.

26. To assemble, use a serrated knife to cut the pastry into 3 rectangles, measuring around 6.5 × 2.7 inches (16.5 × 7cm). This will leave some scraps around the edges. Alternatively, cut it into smaller rectangles and make multiple mille-feuilles.

27. Add the chilled Diplomat Cream to a piping bag fitted with a large round tip nozzle, as well as the Hazelnut Praline Paste to another piping bag with a small hole cut off the end.

28. Taking one of the puff pastry rectangles, pipe the Diplomat Cream in three lines, along the non-caramelized side of the puff pastry. Repeat this on the second rectangle of puff pastry. Then, pipe a thin layer of Hazelnut Praline Paste in between each line of cream.

29. Stack the two rectangles on top of each, then place the final rectangle on top, caramelized side facing out.

30. Carefully flip the mille-feuille onto its side and lift it onto a serving plate. This is best served immediately.

Apple Tarte Tatin

MAKES 6 TARTE TATINS

1 batch Puff Pastry (page 190)

170g granulated/caster sugar

40g unsalted butter, cubed, cold and cubed, plus more for melting

½ fresh vanilla bean

Pinch of sea salt

15 Pink Lady apples

Powdered/icing sugar, for dusting

Vanilla Chantilly (page 224), to serve

This hypnotizing plated dessert is as impressive in taste, as it is looks. The spiralized apples take a lot of attention and detail, but when baked with the caramel, you end up with a spiral of soft, sweet apples. We are using the same puff pastry recipe as the Tier 1 mille-feuille (page 190) but elevating it with this challenging apple filling. All the elements can be prepared ahead of time and chilled, then warmed just before serving.

1. Prepare the puff pastry dough, as per the recipe for the Hazelnut Praline Mille-Feuille (page 190). Once you have performed all 6 folds, chill the dough in the fridge until you are ready to use it.

2. Preheat the oven to 320°F/160°C.

3. To make the caramel, add 25g of sugar to a medium saucepan over medium heat. Allow the sugar to melt until lightly golden. Stir the caramel, then add another 25g of sugar. Stir, then cook until lightly golden. Repeat this process until you've added all the sugar and the caramel is golden.

4. Continue to cook the caramel until it reaches a deep golden color. Remove the saucepan from the heat and add the butter one piece at a time, whisking vigorously between each addition. It's important to add the butter slowly so the caramel emulsifies and doesn't split.

5. Use a knife to cut the vanilla bean lengthwise and scrape the seeds into the saucepan. Add the sea salt and stir well.

6. Take a silicone cylinder mold with 6 cavities of 2.75 inches wide and 1.4 inches deep (7 × 3.5cm). Pour 25g of caramel into each cavity. Work very quickly here or else the caramel will begin to set.

7. Working with one apple at a time, screw it into a vegetable sheet cutter. Use the crank to rotate the apple to create a long, thin strip.

8. Lay out the strip of apple (don't worry if it cracks slightly) and cut the thinner tail ends off (anything with a width less than 1.75 inches [4.5cm]). Roll the strip of apple into itself as tight as possible. If it breaks, just overlap the pieces slightly and continue to roll. Depending on the size of your apples, you'll need strips from roughly 2½ apples to make a spiral big enough to fit the diameter of the mold. Just before you finish rolling the first apple, take the strip from a second apple and overlap them slightly. Continue to roll until you have a tight spiral.

9. Flip the roll of apple so the spiral is now facing up and check to see if it will fit tightly into the cavity of the mold. Add more apple or remove some strips depending on the fit in the mold.

SPECIAL EQUIPMENT

Silicone cylinder mold, 2.75 ×
   1.4-inch (7 × 3.5cm)

Vegetable sheet cutter

2.5-inch (6cm) circular
   cookie cutter

2× perforated baking trays

2× perforated baking mats

Rolling pin

10. Place the roll on its side and use a sharp knife to cut the top and bottom off the roll so you have a clean disk of apple that's about 1.5 inches (4cm) thick. Choose the side of the roll with the "prettiest" spiral and press this face down into the caramel. The apple will shrink as it bakes, so it's important that it's very tight against the side of the mold and peaks just slightly above the rim.

11. Repeat this with the remaining apples. Once you have them all in the mold, brush the tops with a light layer of melted butter.

12. Place the mold on a baking tray and place the tray into the oven. Bake for 40 minutes. During baking, if the apples begin to rise out of the molds as the caramel bubbles, just gently press them back in with a palette knife.

13. Remove the tray from the oven and place a sheet of parchment paper on top of the mold. Place a baking tray on top and a heavy item, such as a pan, on top of the tray. This will compress the apples into the caramel. Place everything in the oven and bake for 40 minutes more.

14. Remove everything from the oven and remove the pan, tray, and paper. Allow the apples to cool at room temperature for 30 minutes before refrigerating for 2 hours. They can also be chilled overnight and used the next day.

15. Preheat the oven to 430°F/220°C.

16. Remove the puff pastry from the fridge. Place the dough on a lightly floured surface and roll it into a rough rectangle, about 0.3 inches (0.8cm) thick. Use a cookie cutter to cut 6 disks from the dough, each about 2.5 inches (6.5cm) wide.

17. Place the disks on a perforated baking tray lined with a perforated baking mat. (Or you can use a sheet of parchment paper). Place a second perforated mat on top along with a baking tray.

18. Place everything in the oven and bake the discs for 10 minutes. Lower the oven temperature to 355°F/180°C and bake for 35-40 minutes more.

19. Remove everything from the oven and remove the mat and tray on top. You'll see that the disks have spread slightly. Use the cookie cutter to carefully cut them down to size again. Place the tray back in the oven and bake the disks for 5–10 minutes more, or until they have a light golden color.

20. Remove the tray from the oven and raise the oven temperature to 390°F/200°C. Dust the disks with a layer of powdered sugar. Place the tray back in the oven and bake the disks until they're a deep golden color. Be very careful not to burn them. Remove the tray from the oven and allow the disks to cool.

21. Carefully remove the caramelized apples from the mold and place them on the puff pastry disks so the "pretty" spiral is facing up. If the disk is bigger than the apple, use a microplane to carefully trim the disk down to size.

22. You can eat these cold or place them in a warm oven (355°F/180°C) for a few minutes to heat them through.

23. Prepare the Vanilla Chantilly. I prefer to use slightly less sugar than the recipe suggests because the apples bring enough sweetness. Spoon the chantilly on the side of the serving plate before serving.

Brioche Feuilletée

MAKES 2 LOAVES

FOR THE BRIOCHE FEUILLETÉE

150g whole milk

85g eggs

17g fresh yeast or 8.5g instant dry yeast

415g all-purpose/plain flour, plus more for dusting

8g sea salt

50g granulated/caster sugar

40g unsalted butter, softened

Nonstick cooking spray, for coating

FOR THE BUTTER BLOCK

250g unsalted butter, slightly softened

FOR THE SYRUP

100g granulated/caster sugar

100g water

While this is a Tier 1 recipe, it is certainly one of the more challenging ones. Laminating dough took me years of practice, but once you've nailed it, it opens you up to a huge repertoire of recipes you can achieve. With this recipe, imagine a classic brioche, with the flakey lamination of a croissant. It is finished with a shiny sugar glaze, which makes the buttery layers pop, and brings a touch of sweetness.

1. Into the bowl of a stand mixer fitted with a dough hook, add the milk, eggs, and yeast. Whisk them to combine.

2. Pour the remaining ingredients for the dough into the bowl, then mix on a medium-low speed for 12–15 minutes, pausing to scrape down the side of the bowl as needed. Initially, the dough will be quite sticky, but it will pull together into a smooth dough.

3. To check the dough is done, remove a very small piece and roll it into a ball. Stretch the ball out gently with your hands, and if you can stretch it without it tearing, and the dough has a "windowpane", it is ready (see page 38).

4. Lift the dough out onto your work surface and use your hands to shape it into a ball. Spray a large bowl with nonstick cooking spray and add the dough. Lightly spray the top of the dough, cover the bowl with plastic wrap/cling film and proof it at room temperature for 1 hour.

5. After 1 hour, remove the dough from the bowl, knock the air out of the dough and then shape it into a ball again. Spray the bowl again with nonstick cooking spray and place it back in the bowl, topping with nonstick cooking spray. Cover the bowl tightly with plastic wrap/cling film and proof for 12 hours in the fridge (it is best to do this overnight).

6. For the butter block, take a large sheet of parchment paper, and place the butter in the center of one half of the paper. Fold the other half of the parchment paper over the top, then fold the edges and sides to create a neat block, about 7 × 8-inches (18 x 20cm). Flip the block over so the folded edges are underneath.

7. Use a rolling pin to roll the butter across the block of parchment paper, ensuring you reach the corners. You should end up with a neat, even block of butter. Place this in the fridge to chill until firm.

8. Before you remove the dough from the fridge, you need to ensure your butter is at the correct temperature to laminate. Too cold and it will crack, too warm and it will leak. Remove it from the fridge and place an instant read thermometer in it, it needs to be around 55–57°F/13–14°C.

Stand mixer, with the dough hook attachment

Rolling pin

Instant read thermometer

2× 1lb loaf tins (7 × 3.5 × 2-inch (18cm × 9cm × 5cm))

9. Once the butter is close to temperature, remove the chilled dough from the fridge and lift it out of the bowl. Lightly flour the work surface and the top of the dough, and use your hands to press the air out of the dough and shape it into a rough square.

10. Roll the dough into a rectangle, roughly 7.5 inches wide, and 18 inches long (19 × 45cm). The butter block should now be at temperature.

11. Place it into the center of the dough, it should fit just perfectly to the width of the dough. Fold the left third of dough into the center of the butter block, then the right third of dough into the center of the butter block, creating a seam where the dough meets.

12. Use your fingers to seal the seam together, and then also seal the edges of dough around the sides together so that the butter is completely encased in the dough.

13. Work quickly here or the butter and dough will become too warm. Lightly flour the dough block and with the seam horizontally in front of you, roll the dough just a few times to give it some slight width. Then rotate the dough 90°, so the seam is now in line with you vertically, and begin to roll the dough out into a long rectangular shape. Don't worry too much about the length of the rectangle, but more about the thickness of it. You want it to be around 0.2–0.25 inches (0.5–0.7mm) thick (or thereabouts). Try to ensure as you are rolling you are keeping it in as neat of a rectangle shape as possible.

14. Dust off any excess flour and then use a pastry wheel just to trim off any small wonky edges so you have a neat rectangle. Then, perform your first single fold (also known as a letter fold). Take the top third of the dough and fold it slightly over halfway. Then take the bottom third of the dough and fold this over the top, just like you are folding a letter.

15. Wrap the dough in plastic wrap and chill it for 30 minutes in the fridge.

16. Remove the chilled dough and lightly flour it. With the exposed edges horizontally in front of you, roll the dough to give it a little width, then turn it 90° so the edges are now in line vertically with you. Roll the dough into a long rectangle as per step 13, perform a single fold, and then chill for 30 minutes. Repeat this one more time, rolling the dough, and performing a final single turn. Chill for 30 minutes.

17. Once the dough has chilled, roll it out again as before, until you have a rectangle shape that is roughly 27.5 × 5.5 inches (70 × 14cm) and 0.31 inch/8mm thick. The thickness is important here.

18. Cut the dough into two long strips, each measuring 27.5 × 2.75 inches (70 × 7cm). Flip the strips onto their side, and then carefully shape them into an accordion-style "S"-shaped zigzag. Lift them into two 1Lb (450g) loaf pans, ensuring there is about a ¼-inch gap between the "S". folds If you feel the dough is too soft when you are trying to shape it, chill the strips for 10–15 minutes in the freezer and then carry on.

19. Lightly cover the top of the pans with plastic wrap and proof them at room temperature for around 4–6 hours. Now, this seems like vague timing, but your room temperature will have a huge impact on how long it takes to proof. The brioche is proofed when the folds of the "S" are now touching each other and the layers look like they are almost splitting slightly.

20. While the dough is proofing, prepare the syrup by adding the sugar and water to a medium saucepan. Place it over medium heat and bring it to a boil, and then continue to cook for a few minutes until it has thickened slightly and is a more syrupy consistency. Set it aside to cool.

21. Just before the dough has proofed, preheat the oven to 430°F/220°C.

22. Place the loaves into the oven and immediately drop the temperature to 365°F/185°C and bake for around 18–20 minutes, or until they are a deep golden color.

23. Carefully remove them from the pans and onto a rack. While they are still warm, use a pastry brush to paint a light layer of syrup over the top and then serve them while they are warm or let them cool.

Tropézienne Cube

MAKES TWO 10-INCH CUBES

FOR THE BRIOCHE FEUILLETÉE

150g whole milk

85g eggs

17g fresh yeast or 8.5g instant dry yeast

415g all-purpose/plain flour

8g sea salt

50g granulated/caster sugar

40g unsalted butter, softened

Nonstick cooking spray, for coating

FOR THE BUTTER BLOCK

250g unsalted butter, slightly softened

½ batch Diplomat Cream (page 211), for filling

The cube! The pièce de résistance of this book, using the Tier 1 Brioche Feuilletée (page 198), but baking it blind in a square tin, resulting in a pastry worthy of the best bakeries in the world. It has a perfect honeycomb center, we finish it by filling it with a rich vanilla Diplomat Cream that is the ultimate, decadent filling.

1. Add the milk, eggs, and yeast to the bowl of a stand mixer and whisk to combine.

2. Pour the remaining ingredients for the dough on top, then place it on a stand mixer fitted with a dough hook.

3. Mix on medium-low speed for 12–15 minutes, pausing to scrape down the side of the bowl as needed. Initially, the dough will be quite sticky, but it will pull together into a smooth dough.

4. To check the dough is done, remove a very small piece and roll it into a ball. Stretch the ball out gently with your hands, and if you can stretch it without it tearing, and the dough has a "windowpane" it is ready (see page 38).

5. Lift the dough out onto your work surface and use your hands to shape it into a ball. Spray a large bowl with nonstick cooking spray and lift the dough in. Lightly spray the top of the dough, cover the bowl with plastic wrap/cling film and proof it at room temperature for 1 hour.

6. After 1 hour, remove the dough from the bowl, knock the air out of it, and then shape it into a ball again. Spray the bowl and the dough again with nonstick cooking spray and place it back in the bowl. Cover the bowl tightly with plastic wrap/cling film and proof for 12 hours in the fridge (it is best to do this overnight).

7. For the butter block, take a large sheet of parchment paper, and place the butter in the center of one-half of the paper. Fold the other half of the parchment paper over the top, then fold the edges and sides to create a neat block, about 7 × 8 inches (18 × 20cm). Flip the block over so the folded edges are underneath.

8. Use a rolling pin to roll the butter across the block of parchment paper, ensuring you reach the corners. You should end up with a neat, even block of butter. Place this in the fridge to chill until firm.

9. Before you remove the dough from the fridge, you need to ensure your butter is at the correct temperature to laminate. Too cold and it will crack, too warm and it will leak. Remove it from the fridge and place an instant read thermometer in it. It needs to be around 55–57°F/13–14°C.

SPECIAL EQUIPMENT

Stand mixer with the whisk attachment and the dough hook attachment

Rolling pin

Instant read thermometer

2× 3.9 × 3.9 × 3.9-inch (10 × 10 × 10cm) square baking pans/ tins, with a removable lid

Piping bag, plus a small round tip nozzle

10. Once the butter is close to temperature, remove the chilled dough from the fridge and lift it out of the bowl. Lightly flour the work surface and the top of the dough, and use your hands to press the air out of the dough and shape it into a rough square.

11. Roll the dough into a rectangle, roughly 7.5 inches wide, and 18 inches long (19 × 46cm). The butter block should now be at temperature.

12. Place it into the center of the dough, it should fit just perfectly to the width of the dough. Fold the left third of dough into the center of the butter block, then the right third of dough into the center of the butter block, creating a seam where the dough meets.

13. Use your fingers to seal the seam together, and then also seal the edges of dough around the sides together so that the butter is completely encased in the dough.

14. Work quickly here or the butter and dough will become too warm. Lightly flour the dough block and with the seam horizontally in front of you, roll the dough just a few times to give it some slight width. Then rotate the dough 90 degrees, so the seam is now in line with your vertically, and begin to roll the dough out into a long rectangular shape. Don't worry too much about the length of the rectangle, but more about the thickness of it. You want it to be around 0.2-0.25-inch (5-7mm) thick (or thereabouts). Try to ensure as you are rolling you are keeping it in as neat of a rectangle shape as possible.

15. Dust off any excess flour and then use a pastry wheel just to trim off any small wonky edges so you have a neat rectangle. Then, perform your first single fold (also known as a letter fold). Take the top third of the dough and fold it slightly over halfway. Then take the bottom third of the dough and fold this over the top—just like you are folding a letter.

16. Wrap the dough in plastic wrap and chill it for 30 minutes in the fridge.

17. Remove the chilled dough and lightly flour it. With the exposed edges horizontally in front of you, roll the dough to give it a little width, then turn it 90° so the edges are now in line vertically with you. Roll the dough into a long rectangle as per step 14, perform a single fold, and then chill for 30 minutes. Repeat this one more time, rolling the dough, and performing a final single turn. Chill for 30 minutes.

18. Once the dough has chilled, roll it out again as before, until you have a rectangle shape, roughly 8.5 inches (22cm) wide and 0.3-inch (7.5mm) thick. Don't worry about the length of the rectangle as we are going to trim this down.

19. Cut the dough into two long strips, each measuring 3.5 inches (9cm).

20. Then, place each strip onto your digital scale and weigh the amount. You want a strip of dough that weighs 260g, so keep cutting some length off the end of the strip until your dough reaches that weight. It is important to work quickly so the dough doesn't get too warm.

21. Lay the strip out, and starting from the short end, roll the dough on itself, into a tight log shape. Lift this, seam-side down, into a 3.9 × 3.9 × 3.9-inch (10 × 10 × 10cm) square baking pan with a removable lid. Repeat this for the second strip of dough.

22. Place the lids on the pans, and proof them at room temperature for around 4–6 hours. Now, this seems like vague timing, but your room temperature will have a huge impact on how long it takes to proof. The cube is proofed when you slide the lid back and the dough has very nearly reached the top of the pan, and there is only about 0.6-inches (1.5cm) of room left. If you underproof the dough, it will not fill the pan as it bakes, so it is important to keep an eye on it.

23. While the dough is proving—it is a good time to prepare the crème pâtissierè for the Diplomat Cream, so that this can chill (page 211).

24. Preheat your oven to 430°F/220°C. Once the cube has proofed, place it into the oven, with the lid on. Drop the oven temperature to 375°F/190°C and bake for 35 minutes.

25. Once baked, immediately remove them from the oven and tip them out of the pans onto a rack. Do not leave them in the pans or the residual steam will cause it to collapse slightly. Allow them to cool for 1 hour. The brioches can be wrapped in plastic wrap and stored at room temperature if you are not ready to fill them, but they will lose some of the flakiness. When you are ready to serve them, it is best to reheat them in a 345°F/175°C oven, for 5–10m or until they feels flaky again. Let them cool for a few minutes before filling them.

26. Remove the crème pâtissierè for the diplomat cream from the fridge and whisk the whipped cream. Fold the cream through the crème pâtissierè and then add the mixture into a piping bag fitted with a small round tip nozzle.

27. Poke a hole into the bottom of the brioche cube using a small knife and then pipe the Diplomat Cream inside, until it feels heavy. Repeat with the second cube. These are best served immediately.

CHAPTER 7

essentials

Crème Anglaise

115g egg yolks
40g granulated/caster sugar
Pinch sea salt
250g heavy/double cream
125g whole milk
1 fresh vanilla bean

SPECIAL EQUIPMENT
Instant read thermometer

The perfect sauce to serve warm with winter crumbles or poured over a chocolate soufflé. Use fresh vanilla beans for the best taste.

1. Add the egg yolks, sugar and salt to a medium bowl and whisk together for 1–2 minutes until pale and smooth.

2. Meanwhile, scrape the seeds from the vanilla bean and add these into a medium saucepan along with the cream and milk. Place this over medium heat.

3. Once steaming, slowly pour it over the egg yolk mixture, whisking constantly so that they don't scramble.

4. Pour this back into the pan and continue to cook, stirring constantly until it is thick enough to coat the back of a spoon, and reaches a temperature of roughly 176–185°F/80–85°C.

5. Immediately pass it through a sieve on top of a small bowl. The crème anglaise can be used immediately.

Chocolate Crémeux

200g dark chocolate, 70% cocoa solids, chopped

120g eggs

5g granulated/caster sugar

150g whole milk

150g heavy/double cream

SPECIAL EQUIPMENT

Instant read thermometer

Hand blender

Creméux translates as "creamy" in French and this is exactly that—a thick, decadent chocolate cream. Once it has chilled it doesn't need to be whipped, so it can be piped or quenelled and served as an accompaniment with a plated dessert. It is slightly less stable compared to chocolate whipped ganache, so be careful not to overwork it too much.

1. Chop the chocolate into small pieces and add this to a tall measuring jug and set aside.

2. In a large bowl, combine the eggs, sugar, milk, and cream.

3. Place the bowl over a pot of gently simmering water, ensuring the bowl doesn't touch the water, and whisk constantly. You're looking for the mixture to thicken and reach a temperature of about 167°F/75°C.

4. Immediately pour the mixture through a sieve over the jug/cup of chopped chocolate.

5. Allow the mixture to sit for 2 minutes, then use a hand blender to blend until smooth.

6. Pour the mixture into a container and refrigerate for 6 hours or overnight.

7. Remove it from the fridge and then it is ready to use.

Crème Pâtissière

500g whole milk
1 fresh vanilla bean
75g granulated/caster sugar
120g egg yolks
40g cornstarch/corn flour
Pinch of sea salt
45g unsalted butter, cold

A staple in French baking recipes and a fundamental technique to learn. It is a rich vanilla cream that is ideal for filling rather than piping and can be used for mille-feuille, chocolate éclairs, and donuts.

1. In a medium saucepan on the stovetop over medium heat, add the milk. Cut the vanilla bean bean lengthways and scrape out the seeds into the saucepan. Heat the mixture until it just begins to steam.

2. Remove it from the heat and place a lid on the saucepan, allowing the vanilla to infuse for 20 minutes.

3. In a separate medium bowl, whisk together the sugar, egg yolks, cornstarch, and salt until smooth and thickened.

4. Place the milk mixture back on the heat until it is just steaming. Slowly pour this mixture over the sugar and eggs mixture, whisking constantly to prevent the eggs from scrambling.

5. Pour the mixture back into the saucepan. Whisk constantly over medium heat until it begins to bubble, then cook for 1 minute.

6. Remove the saucepan from the heat and pass the mixture through a sieve placed over a large bowl.

7. Whisk in the butter until the mixture is smooth. Cover the bowl with plastic wrap/cling film and refrigerate for 4–6 hours or overnight.

8. Once chilled, whisk the crème pâtissière until smooth and use immediately.

Diplomat Cream

2g powdered gelatin, plus 12g cold water

250ml whole milk

½ fresh vanilla bean or 1 tsp vanilla bean paste

60g egg yolks

Pinch sea salt

40g granulated/caster sugar

20g cornstarch/corn flour

25g unsalted butter, cold and cubed

200g heavy/double cream

A simple combination of crème pâtissierè with whipped cream folded through. This is a great filling for any choux pastry or used in a fraisier cake. It pairs perfectly with any kind of summer berry dessert.

1. Add the gelatin and cold water to a saucepan and let it bloom for 5 minutes.

2. Into a medium saucepan, add the milk along with the scraped seeds from a fresh vanilla bean. Place the pan on a medium heat until it is steaming.

3. While the milk mixture is heating up, add the egg yolks, salt, sugar, and cornstarch to a bowl. Whisk for 1–2 minutes until pale and thick.

4. Remove the hot milk from the heat, and slowly pour it over the egg yolks, whisking constantly. Add just a small amount at a time so that the egg yolks don't scramble. Once it is all incorporated, pour the mixture back into the pan and place it on the heat.

5. Heat the mixture, whisking constantly until it starts to bubble. Once it does, cook for a further 1 minute.

6. Pour the mixture through a fine-mesh sieve over a clean bowl and scrape the mixture through using a spatula. Add the bloomed gelatin into a small pan and melt it gently over a low heat.

7. Add the butter and melted gelatin to the milk mixture. Whisk it until the butter has melted and the mixture is smooth.

8. Place a sheet of plastic wrap/cling film directly on the surface and chill it in the fridge overnight or for 6 hours minimum.

9. Once chilled, whisk the mixture to smooth it out. Add the cream to a medium bowl and whisk it to a medium-soft peak. Fold the cream into the crème pâtissierè base in three parts until it is completely smooth. The cream is now ready to use.

Lemon Curd

6g lemon zest
200g fresh lemon juice
180g caster sugar
200g eggs
300g unsalted butter,
  softened

SPECIAL EQUIPMENT

Instant read thermometer
Hand blender

Slightly different to a classic lemon curd, this has more butter, giving it a thicker, creamier consistency. I love to use this as a filling in a lemon layer cake with swiss meringue buttercream or piped on the side of a plated dessert.

1. In a large bowl, combine the lemon zest, lemon juice, sugar, and eggs. Whisk together to combine.

2. Place the bowl over a pot of gently simmering water, ensuring the bowl doesn't touch the water, and whisk the ingredients constantly. Keep whisking the mixture until it's thickened. It should reach a temperature of about 167–176°F/75–80°C)

3. Remove the bowl from the pot and pass the mixture through a sieve, on top of a tall measuring jug/cup.

4. Allow the mixture to cool to 104°F/40°C, then use a hand blender to blend in the butter a little at a time until a thick, buttery curd forms.

5. Pour the curd into a sterilized jar. Seal and refrigerate for up to 1 week.

Salted Caramel

45g whole milk
175g heavy/double cream
135g glucose syrup, divided
80g granulated/caster sugar
1.5g flaky sea salt
60g unsalted butter

Using glucose is the secret here, as it helps to prevent crystallization and keeps the caramel so soft. It's ideal for swirling into brownie batter or drizzled-over ice cream. For a twist on the classic, try infusing the cream with any of your favorite spices.

1. In a medium saucepan on the stovetop over medium heat, combine the milk, cream, and 45g of glucose syrup. Bring to a gentle simmer, whisking the mixture to ensure the syrup has fully dissolved. Remove the saucepan from the heat but ensure the mixture stays warm.

2. In a medium saucepan on the stovetop over medium heat, combine the sugar and the remaining 90g of glucose syrup. Cook until the mixture turns a deep caramel color, but try to avoid stirring the mixture. Shake the saucepan to help disperse the sugar. If the sugar isn't breaking down, give it a quick stir with a spatula.

3. Once golden, immediately pour in the hot cream mixture, being very careful as it will bubble up violently. Whisk the mixture and cook for 1 minute.

4. Remove the saucepan from the heat and pour the mixture through a sieve and into a large bowl. Let the mixture cool for 2 minutes. Add the sea salt flakes and butter. Blend or whisk until smooth.

5. Pour the mixture into an air-tight container and store at room temperature.

Vanilla Mascarpone Cream

3g powdered gelatin

18g cold water

300g heavy/double cream

15g granulated/caster sugar

1 vanilla pod or 1 tsp vanilla
  bean paste

100g mascarpone

SPECIAL EQUIPMENT

Hand blender

Stand mixer, with the
  whisk attachment

While this cream is similar in taste and texture to a classic chantilly cream, the addition of gelatin and mascarpone gives it more stability, making it much easier to pipe.

1. Into a small bowl, add the powdered gelatin and cold water. Stir them together to fully combine then allow it to bloom for 5 minutes.

2. Add the cream and sugar to a medium saucepan. Using a knife, make a lengthwise cut in the vanilla bean, then scrape the seeds into the cream and stir. If using vanilla bean paste instead, stir this into the cream.

3. Place the saucepan over medium heat, stirring occasionally until the cream is steaming, but not boiling.

4. Remove the pan from the heat and stir in the bloomed gelatin until it has fully dissolved.

5. Into a tall, heat-proof measuring jug/cup, add the mascarpone, then pour the hot cream over the top.

6. Use a hand blender to blend this together until smooth. Pour it into a medium bowl and place a sheet of plastic wrap/cling wrap directly on the surface. Refrigerate it for a minimum of 6 hours, or ideally overnight.

7. Add the chilled cream into the bowl of a stand mixer fitted with a whisk attachment. Whisk on a medium speed until it reaches a medium peak.

Swiss Meringue Buttercream

2 vanilla beans or 2 tsp
vanilla bean paste

400g egg whites

745g granulated/caster sugar

7g sea salt, plus more
if needed

1000g unsalted butter, room
temperature

SPECIAL EQUIPMENT

Instant read thermometer

Stand mixer, with the whisk
attachment and the
paddle attachment

My go-to buttercream for all of my layer cakes. Swiss meringue is lighter and has less sweetness compared to a classic American buttercream. The texture means it is perfect for filling cakes, but also has a great consistency for detailed piping work. There is lots of butter, so be careful when using it in hot conditions! Play around with the salt and vanilla levels to your liking.

1. If you're using vanilla beans, use a knife to cut the beans lengthwise and scrape the seeds into the bowl of a stand mixer. Add the egg whites, sugar, and salt.

2. Place the bowl over a pan of gently simmering water. Whisk the mixture constantly until it reaches 150°F/65°C.

3. Remove the bowl from the heat and place it on the stand mixer fitted with the whisk attachment. Whisk on medium for 8–10 minutes, or until the bowl feels cool to the touch. It's really important for the meringue to cool completely before adding the butter.

4. Slowly add the butter a piece at a time. Initially, the mixture might look quite soupy, then as you add more butter, it might look curdled. This is completely normal. Once you've added all the butter, keep whisking until smooth. This could take a few minutes.

5. Switch to the paddle attachment and mix it on a low speed for 1–2 minutes to get rid of any air bubbles. Taste the buttercream and add in more salt or vanilla if needed, until it reaches your desired flavor. Use immediately.

Chocolate Swiss Meringue Buttercream

1 batch Vanilla Swiss
   Meringue Buttercream
   (page 219)

200g dark chocolate, 70%
   cocoa solids, chopped

SPECIAL EQUIPMENT

Stand mixer, with the
   whisk attachment

There isn't really a recipe to follow here, just pour in lots of melted chocolate until you are happy with the taste!

1. Prepare the Vanilla Swiss Meringue Buttercream as per the recipe on page 219.

2. Add the chocolate into a medium bowl, and place it over a saucepan of gently simmering water. Keep stirring it with a spatula until it has completely melted.

3. Remove it from the heat. The chocolate needs to be fluid but not hot, so it needs to cool for around 5 minutes at room temperature.

4. Once you have added all the butter to your buttercream and it is smooth, slowly drizzle in the cooled melted chocolate.

5. Keep whisking until you have a smooth chocolate buttercream. You can also add more melted chocolate depending on your taste preference.

Whipped Vanilla Ganache

4g powdered gelatin

24g cold water

380g heavy/double cream

1 fresh vanilla bean or 1 tsp vanilla bean paste

130g white chocolate, chopped

SPECIAL EQUIPMENT

Hand blender

Stand mixer, with the whisk attachment

What I like to call "dream cream" because of how stable it is. The addition of gelatin provides stability, which means it holds its shape extremely well, perfect for piping. The white chocolate means it is slightly on the sweeter side so it's ideal for balancing out desserts such as the Triple Chocolate Brownie Fingers (page 70).

1. Place the powdered gelatin into a small bowl along with the cold water. Allow it to bloom for 5 minutes.

2. Add the cream into a saucepan along with the seeds from a fresh vanilla bean (or vanilla bean paste). Place it over a medium heat and stir until the mixture is steaming but not boiling.

3. Place the chopped chocolate in a tall measuring jug/cup and pour the cream over the top. Scoop in the bloomed gelatin.

4. Take a hand blender, and blend the mixture until it is smooth. Pour the mixture into a bowl and cover the surface with the plastic wrap/cling film. Place it in the fridge overnight.

5. Once chilled, add the mixture into a stand mixer fitted with a whisk attachment. Whisk on a medium speed until you have a medium peak. Add it into a piping bag and use immediately.

Whipped Chocolate Ganache

3g powdered gelatin

18g cold water

120g dark chocolate, 70% cocoa solids

500g double/heavy cream

SPECIAL EQUIPMENT

Hand blender

Stand mixer, with the whisk attachment

The chocolate version of "dream cream"—bringing less sweetness compared to the vanilla version, but just as stable to pipe. This can easily be used in place of chocolate namelaka or chocolate chantilly throughout the book.

1. Into a small bowl, add the powdered gelatin and pour the cold water over the top. Stir it together and then allow it to bloom for 5 minutes.

2. Meanwhile, add the chocolate to a bowl, and place this over a pan of gently simmering water. Stir this until it is completely melted, then remove it from the heat and set it to one side.

3. Add the cream into a medium saucepan and place it over a medium heat. Once it is steaming, but not boiling, remove it from the heat and scoop in the bloomed gelatin. Stir this through until it has completely dissolved.

4. Using a rubber spatula, stir the center of the melted chocolate in small circular motions, slowly pouring in the hot cream. Initially it may look slightly split but it will pull together. If you have a hand blender, once you have added all the cream, give it a quick blend to fully emulsify it.

5. Place a sheet of plastic wrap/cling film directly on the surface and chill it for a minimum of 6 hours or overnight in the fridge.

6. Once chilled, use a hand whisk with gently whisk the ganache until you reach a medium peak.

Vanilla Chantilly

300g heavy/double cream, cold

10-20g powdered/icing sugar, to taste

1 fresh vanilla bean or 1 tsp vanilla bean paste

SPECIAL EQUIPMENT

Stand mixer, with the whisk attachment

A classic cream that goes with almost every dessert. Adjust the sweetness levels to your preference and be careful not to over-whip it.

1. Into the bowl of a stand mixer fitted with a whisk attachment, add the cream, sugar (you can adjust the sweetness levels to your taste), and the seeds from a fresh vanilla bean or the vanilla bean paste.

2. Whisk the mixture on medium speed until it reaches a medium-soft peak. The cream is ready to use.

Pistachio Praline Paste

150g shelled pistachios
40g granulated/caster sugar
Pinch of flaky sea salt
40–60g vegetable oil

SPECIAL EQUIPMENT
Baking tray/sheet
Silicone baking mat
Food processor

With slightly less sweetness than the Hazelnut Praline Paste (page 227), this has an amazing vibrant color and can be used as a decorative finish to desserts (try piping it on the Pistachio and Orange Viennese Whirls (page 133)!) Look out for bright-green skinned pistachios to achieve the best color.

1. Take the shelled pistachios and place them onto a baking tray lined with a silicone mat. To get the best color for your praline, you want to use vibrant green pistachios.

2. Meanwhile, into a shallow frying pan, add ⅓ of the sugar and melt it over low heat without stirring/shaking the pan, if needed, to disperse the sugar.

3. Once melted, add the second ⅓ of sugar and gently stir it together. Once that has melted, add the remaining sugar and keep stirring it until you have a deep caramel color.

4. Immediately remove it from the heat and pour it over your pistachios. Add a pinch of flaky salt and let it set for 30 minutes at room temperature, until the caramel is solid.

5. Break the praline into pieces and add it to a high-powered food processor. Blend it on medium speed, slowly drizzling in the oil. Depending on the thickness you would like, you can adjust the amount of oil needed.

6. Scrape down the sides of the blender as needed until you have a smooth paste. Store it in an airtight container.

Hazelnut Praline Paste

1 vanilla bean (optional)

230g granulated/caster sugar

70g water

350g whole roasted hazelnuts, without skins

Pinch of flaky sea salt

SPECIAL EQUIPMENT

Instant read thermometer

Baking tray/sheet

Silicone baking mat

Food processor

A staple in so much french pastry, hazelnut praline gives you a deep nutty caramelized paste that can be folded through creams or frozen and used as inserts for decorative entremets. Try adjusting how deep you roast the hazelnuts for different flavor profiles.

1. Use a knife to cut the vanilla bean (if using) lengthwise and scrape the seeds into a small bowl. Set aside.

2. In a medium saucepan over medium heat, combine the sugar and water. Heat the mixture until it reaches 230°F/110°C.

3. Add the hazelnuts and the vanilla seeds. Stir constantly with a spatula. The mixture will initially look quite clumpy, then the sugar will crystallize, but eventually, as you keep stirring, the sugars will caramelize and you should have a deep golden caramel surrounding the nuts. This will take about 3–5 minutes.

4. Immediately remove the saucepan from the heat and transfer the caramelized nuts onto a baking tray lined with a silicone mat. Sprinkle a pinch of sea salt flakes over the top and allow the nuts to set completely at room temperature for 30 minutes.

5. When ready, the praline should be completely cool and solid to the touch. Break it into pieces and add it to a high-powered food processor. Blend for 3–4 minutes on high, scraping down the sides every so often, until you have a smooth, nutty paste. Store in an airtight container for a week at room temperature.

Tuile

MAKES 300G OF TUILE BATTER

60g powdered/icing sugar

75g unsalted butter, melted

75g all-purpose/plain flour

15g honey

75g egg whites, room
  temperature

SPECIAL EQUIPMENT

Stand mixer, with the
  paddle attachment

Silicone tuile mold

Tuile molds come in a huge variety of designs and are the perfect way to add a little crunch and decorative touch to a plated dessert. Once they're baked, it's important to remove them from the mold quickly. You can also set them over a rolling pin while warm to give them a curved effect.

1. Preheat the oven to 330°F/165°C.

2. Add the sugar and melted butter into the bowl of a stand mixer fitted with the paddle attachment. Beat on a medium speed until smooth.

3. Add in the flour and mix again until there are no more dry bits.

4. Finally, add the honey and egg whites and beat until it forms a smooth paste, pausing to scrape down the sides of the bowl as needed.

5. The paste can be spread onto a silicone tuile mold or spread out thinly onto a silicone mat in your desired shape.

6. Bake for 12–14 minutes, depending on your mold/shape, until it is an even golden color.

Index

Acknowledgments

When I started writing this book, I had a pretty overwhelming feeling that I had a lot of work to accomplish on my own, but little did I know there was going to be a whole host of people behind the scenes, taking care of things in life and for the book, which allowed me to really focus. Without them, this book definitely wouldn't be where it is today!

First to my wife Sacha—writing a book is time-consuming enough, but starting this process just 3 months after we had our first baby—I couldn't appreciate your patience any more. There were some tense times, but hopefully the endless supply of cakes coming through the kitchen helped! You've supported me in more ways than you know from day one of my baking journey. You allowed me to quit my job and pursue my dream and I'll forever be grateful.

... Ruben, I hope you can be proud of this when you grow up and if there is one thing you need to carry through your legacy—it's the lemon tart. A must-know recipe for every Adlard!

... My entire family—Mum, Dad, Lucy, Tom, and the girls. I feel like I disappeared for a year writing this but thank you for being my willing taste testers, especially the girls who always gave rave reviews to boost my ego.

... My food stylists, Holly and Lucy. Baking is an art, but making food look good for a camera is a whole other skill. Thank you for calming me when soufflés wouldn't rise and coming up with a solution for every hurdle we faced. You truly made the food shine.

... Sam Harris for his photography. I had such a clear vision of how I wanted the book to look and you blew my expectations away. It was a real honor to watch you work and admire the attention to detail you had for every image.

... My entire team at DK. A book always seemed like a distant goal, but you took a chance on me and my vision. You let me run with my ideas and thankfully said there wasn't too much chocolate! Molly, for tirelessly editing everything and pulling together what seemed like a maze of word documents into a cohesive, stunning book. Cara and Max, for seamlessly helping to organize shoots and answering my never-ending questions on set. Jessica, for your sleek design skills and for bearing with my relentless requests to change things.

And finally to my followers—it's cliché to say it, but all of this truly isn't possible without you. Life is busy and I can't thank you enough for taking time out of your day to engage with my photos and videos, and supporting me year after year. Giving me opportunities like this to write my very own cookbook is something I will forever be grateful for. I hope I've done you justice and you'll enjoy soaking in the recipes from the book. I genuinely enjoy speaking to you on a daily basis, and seeing the creations you come up with. Hopefully this is just the beginning of our journey.